Tomorrow is Another Country

Tomorrow is Another Country: What is wrong with UK's asylum policy?

Myles Harris

Complementary essay by
David Conway

Civitas: Institute for the Study of Civil Society
London

First published January 2003
Civitas
The Mezzanine, Elizabeth House
39 York Road, London SE1 7NQ
email: books@civitas.org.uk

ISBN 1-903 386-25-X

Typeset by Civitas
in New Century Schoolbook

Printed in Great Britain by
Hartington Fine Arts Ltd
Lancing, Sussex

Contents

Authors

Myles Harris is a doctor and a journalist. He lived in the Third World for many years where he witnessed many of the forces that drive immigration. He worked in a black mission hospital in South Africa under apartheid, in the West Indies, and, in 1984, he worked in Ethiopia during the famine for the League of the Red Cross. He has also worked in Papua New Guinea. He has travelled extensively in the Middle East and India. He has written for the *Spectator*, the *Evening Standard*, the *Daily Telegraph*, and the *Daily Mail*. He has published monographs on the collapse of nursing in the UK, the uselessness of counselling and, in 1987, a book, *Breakfast in Hell*, which gave an account of the failure of aid in the Ethiopian famine. He lives in London.

David Conway is Senior Research Fellow in Theology and Religious Studies at University of Surrey Roehampton and Emeritus Professor of Philosophy at Middlesex University. His publications include *A Farewell to Marx*, Penguin Books, 1987; *Classical Liberalism: The Unvanquished Ideal*, Macmillan, 1995; *Free-Market Feminism*, IEA Health and Welfare Unit, 1998 and *The Rediscovery of Wisdom*, Macmillan, 2000.

Foreword

This is the second Civitas book in the last few weeks which has had to begin with a defence of its very publication. The first was *Do We Need Mass Immigration?*, by *The Times'* journalist, Anthony Browne. His painstaking and scholarly efforts to encourage an informed debate about immigration led to an emotional outburst by the Home Secretary, David Blunkett, in the House of Commons. Mr Blunkett said that comment by Anthony Browne in *The Times* 'borders on fascism', an extraordinary remark that Mr Blunkett ought to withdraw, even at this late stage. It has correctly been called McCarthyite, because it was an accusation made with the intention of damaging the reputation of another person without offering even the slightest supporting evidence. Anthony Browne anticipated that less scrupulous critics would resort to false accusations of racism and devoted a section of his book to explaining why such abuse should not be allowed to suppress a free and open debate. Mr Blunkett, who has a whole government department ready and able to do the research work necessary to mount a reasoned defence of his views, should have known better.

Tomorrow is Another Country, by Myles Harris, tackles Britain's asylum system. Just as a reasonable person could be against increased immigration without being personally hostile to any particular immigrants, so a reasonable person could also wish to reform abuse of the asylum system without being hostile to any particular asylum seekers. As Myles Harris argues, we should protect people who are genuinely in fear of their lives, but the asylum system should not become a method of circumventing immigration rules.

No doubt, Myles Harris can look forward to his share of the false accusations that surround the immigration and asylum debate. The favourite epithet—racist—is an effective insult, however, only because the vast majority of people in Britain would not dream of being racist and would be very upset if anyone else even *thought* they might be.

This country is not in any serious danger of becoming racist. The greater risk is that legitimate debate will be suppressed by campaigns of intellectual intimidation.

Name-calling should not discourage a calm, measured and factual debate. We urgently need to lower the temperature and focus on the simple facts, without fear or favour. Myles Harris has provided much new evidence on which an informed public debate can now be based.

David G. Green

1

Why do they come?

Imagine you are up to your ears in debt. Everything you own is mortgaged to money lenders. One of your children is seriously ill but you have no money to pay for her treatment. Your business was recently seized by a drugs cartel which forced you off the premises at gun point while the local police stood laughing on the pavement.

Then you hear of a country which will give you sufficient money to cover all your debts, offer safety and security to you and your immediate family, give you free health care, provide you with a house that is a palace compared with the one in which you live. Even better, your children will bring in time the inestimable benefit of citizenship of the new country, which in a few years will become a valuable commodity that can be traded through arranged marriages to people back home.

All you have to do is to get there. But it is far away and it would take five years of back-breaking work to earn enough for the fare.

It seems hopeless until a friend suggests going to the gang who seized your property. They operate a people-smuggling operation as well as running drugs. If you go into debt for double the sum you already owe, they will get you to this new country.

They will provide you with the false papers, a route and the couriers to get you to anywhere in the world. They run a highly sophisticated operation that takes account of all the twists and turns of Western governments' attempts to keep migrants out. There are a huge variety of ways of getting into Britain, from arriving as a student with a set of perfectly authentic entry papers, but based on a lie, to the crude but much less favoured method these days of trying to board a British truck somewhere in France.[1]

It will be a straightforward mortgage, with one of your family remaining behind as security. The repayment terms are that you hand over everything you earn in the new country to them for the next five years. If you fail to repay your debt, you, or a family member you have left behind, will be killed. Everybody knows that the gangs mean what they say.

> The parents of Gao Liquin owed $30,000 to Fujian money lenders for sending their daughter from China to the US in 1994. A year later they received a terrifying phone call from gang members who had kidnapped her from her New York home demanding $38,000. ... the kidnapping went horribly wrong as the gang members panicked, sensing the police were closing in. Days later, with only a fraction of the ransom paid, Ms Gao was found dead. She had been raped, tortured and beaten, then finally strangled.[2]

One such country that will pay all your debts is Britain. It will provide pocket money, health care and lawyers. The average cost in the first year of a refugee arriving in Britain is £20,000. All of it is funded by the taxpayer.[3]

This will be enough to give our asylum seeker a head start. Even better, the gangs tell him he can work while he is being paid. There are rules about asylum seekers not working, but the British are so rich they do not bother to check on these things. With two incomes you can pay back the gang and still afford to live.

Most migrants are like this man. He is not fleeing political persecution but the persecution that comes with poverty. He is not destitute, otherwise the gangs would not have lent him money. The destitute live in slums in Bombay, Calcutta or Jakarta. Such people can never come to Britain. If you want to find potential political refugees, go to a Burmese jail or a slave factory in China. They cannot leave. Modern asylum seeking is, to all intents and purposes, economic. Asylum seekers are fleeing poverty. They are leaving countries that do not work, that have no laws, for ones that do.

Last year we know of at least 88,300 asylum seekers who knocked on our door.[4] They were from all over the world. Except for a very few, they all have one thing in common:

they will have bought their way here. Some may have beggared themselves to do so. The journey to the West is not cheap. The price varies, from £6,000 to leave Sri Lanka to £20,000 to get out of China.

Only nine per cent of men and 13 per cent of women are granted asylum.[5] The rest present cases to immigration officers which in the main are simply concocted or only the vaguest approximation to the truth. Refugees come in pursuit of the rule of law, but the majority start out by breaking it the moment they set foot on English soil. For, although nobody is prosecuted for trying to obtain money by deception, entering Britain with a concocted story is an attempt to obtain public funds under false pretences, funds that millions have worked to contribute to.

Asylum seekers may intend to work and pay taxes later, but, by failing to tell the truth, they undermine the whole basis of the charitable compact we offer. Moreover, what private insurance fund could sustain an assault on its reserves like this without going bankrupt?

Nor has the true extent of this mass settlement—which for want of a better phrase is called asylum seeking—being made clear to the public. Looking at the graph below tracing the rise in asylum seeking, you could be forgiven for thinking that the number of refugees in 2001 was around 71,400. But this number only applies to heads of families. Although many asylum seekers are single young men, if we add family members, this brings the total number to 92,000.[6] Over and above that, of which we know nothing, are thousands of people who smuggle themselves into Britain completely unseen.

> Based upon the day-to-day experience of the Immigration Service Union members, a very modest estimate would be that, for every person known to attempt to or succeed in entering the UK illegally, two others succeed unnoticed.[7]

More will come. For 'asylum' is a bargain that is repeated every year, offered to more and more people, and will go on being offered until the asylum system is either reformed or abandoned. 'I love this land,' said one Afghan refugee kissing the ground at Dover. 'Fair play, football, David Beckham, nice police.'[8]

Figure 1
Outcome of Asylum Appeals sent to the Adjudicator, 2001

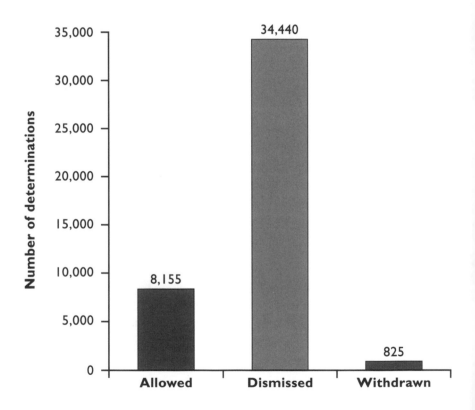

Source: Heath, T. and Hill, R., *Asylum Statistics United Kingdom 2001*, The Home Office Research Development and Statistics Directorate (National Statistics) 31 July 2002, p. 8, fig. 10.

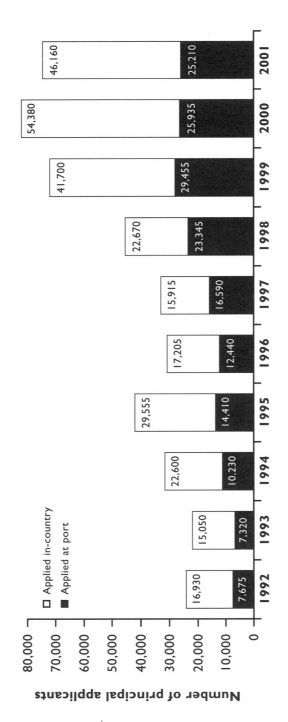

Figure 2
Applications* for Asylum in the United Kingdom by
Location of Application, 1992 -2001

Note: * Excluding dependants
Source: Heath, T. and Hill, R., *Asylum Statistics United Kingdom 2001*, The Home Office Research Development
and Statistics Directorate (National Statistics) 31 July 2002, figure 1.
http://www.homeoffice.gov.uk/rds/immigration1.html

We have always taken refugees. Over the centuries, visionaries, cranks, inventors, scientists, philosophers, plotters, anarchists, communists, fascists, those of every shade of dissident opinion, have found their way to our shores. Tides of refugees bring with them not just ordinary people, but extraordinary ones. Sir Nikolaus Pevsner, whose *Buildings of England* series represents an unrivalled achievement in architectural history, came to this country as a refugee from Nazism, as did Sir Ernst Chain, whose work on the process by which large quantities of penicillin could be manufactured was one of the greatest practical discoveries in the history of medicine. Freud spent his last years in Hampstead; Karl Popper, who came here from Austria, wrote *The Open Society and its Enemies*, defining the nature of a free society.[9] But migration is a mixed blessing. The world's greatest mass killer, Stalin, briefly hid from the Tsarist secret police in London. The murderous Lenin lived in exile in Britain from 1902-1903. Karl Marx, who ruined whole nations with his economic theory, fled to England from France.

2

The Human Rights Act and the surrender of our borders

Britain was, and is, a safe country. There is a law of *habeas corpus*, you do not have to carry your passport when you go out to the shops, and parliament is sovereign. We have a queen but we make our own laws. We police our own borders.

That was until 2 October 2000, when the Labour government passed the Human Rights Act. It incorporated into domestic law the provisions of the European Convention on Human Rights. The passing of the Human Rights Act (which went largely unnoticed outside political and legal circles) had the effect in practice of surrendering our right to decide who could and who could not enter the United Kingdom.

Created in 1950 by the Council of Europe, the European Convention on Human Rights was originally intended to help refugees fleeing Soviet tyranny. It conferred on all human beings the right to free assembly, free speech, religious and political freedom, and freedom from sexual and racial persecution. It gave people the right to travel and the right to due legal process. It was modified in 1958 to apply to refugees from all over the world, especially those from Africa.

In practice only Western governments enforce human rights legislation. Few Third World governments, even those who have signed a human rights convention, would contemplate allowing any of their citizens the following liberties, guaranteed by the Human Rights Act:

7

Article 6 (1)   A fair and public hearing within a reasonable time by
                  an independent and impartial tribunal established by
                  law ...

Article 8 (1)   Everyone has the right to respect for his private and
                  family life, his home and his correspondence

Article 11 (1)   Everyone has the right to freedom of peaceful assembly
                  and to freedom of association with others, including the
                  right to form and to join trade unions for the protection
                  of his interests

The Act sets up an ideal standard of citizenship to which all nations should aspire. If somebody cannot enjoy those rights in his own country, but can reach a country where those rights are upheld, he can make a claim to remain there. In essence, it is a transfer of residence. It gives everybody in the world another country. It creates a superogatory citizenship that allows people to leave countries that do not work and enter countries that do.

Until October 2000, while we were signatories to the European Convention on Human Rights, it remained the province of a foreign court, the European Court of Human Rights in Strasbourg. People went there to have cases heard under its provisions. It was on the whole about generalities. We were guided by it, judges wrote their decisions with their minds on it, but we still had sovereignty over our borders.

But by passing the Human Rights Act, and thus adding the provisions of the Convention to our statute books, the Labour government threw the legal equivalent of a can of petrol onto the flames of mass migration. Unlike our statute and common law, the Human Rights Act is a victim's act. It is about reparation, compensation and rights. The victim discovers he has been wronged and goes to a lawyer to seek redress. Like a giant legal amoeba, it is self-propagating. More and more rights are discovered by the day. A family of Lithuanian asylum seekers brought a High Court claim for damages against Southwark council under the Human Rights Act. They claimed that their human rights had been breached because the house they had left behind in Lithuania had an orchard, but they had been given a flat with no garden in a block scheduled for demolition. They lost their action, but the fact that such a claim was considered by the court shows how much the concept of human rights has broadened since the Convention was drafted to keep people out of gulags.[1] Nor does the Human Rights Act stop at our borders: we have to consider infringements of human rights overseas, with enormous implications for the control of our borders.

Lawyers claim that we still have jurisidiction within our borders. Lord Woolf, the Lord Chief Justice, delivering the 'Thank Offering to Britain' lecture, sponsored by Jewish refugees who fled the Holocaust, said that under the Human Rights Act the courts were only required to 'take account' of the decisions of the Strasbourg court.[2] However, it is extremely hard to conceive of a situation in which a British court would overturn a Strasbourg decision on human rights. Would a British court, for example, rule against the right to a fair trial?

It was almost inevitable, from time to time, Lord Woolf said, that parliament or the government would not strike the right balance between the rights of society and the rights of the individual. Now that the Human Rights Act was in force, however, the courts could act as a long stop. He spoke of the need for the courts to protect the rights of individuals or minorities 'when the tabloids were in full cry', and said that the fact that human rights could not be directly enforced as part of English law in the past meant that our form of democratic government was more vulnerable that it is now to the contravention of those rights.

There is now every prospect of courts seizing their chance to overturn immigration law which does not elevate the rights of ordinary asylum seekers over the host state. For example, if you send somebody back to a country where justice is rudimentary, you could be breaching their human rights.

But who are we to say what standard of justice we should expect in a foreign court? Are we the rulers of these countries and, if we pronounce on their laws, should we not take steps to enforce the decisions of our courts on them? This nonsensical position does not worry lawyers, who spend many profitable hours arguing whether a particular country applies a reasonable standard of justice, or whether individuals are at particular risk.

The idea that our courts should rule on all matters to do with immigration is also backed by MPs and peers on the Joint Committee on Human Rights. In June 2002 they voiced grave concern about a proposal in Mr Blunkett's Asylum and Immigration Bill to have asylum seekers arbitrarily removed whose claims were 'manifestly unfounded'.[3]

'It should not be possible', said the committee, 'to remove a person before he or she has had the opportunity to challenge before an independent tribunal the Secretary of State's certificate that the person's claim to have had a convention right violated is clearly unfounded.'

This means that we have to admit asylum seekers to have their cases heard—however implausible. Many, of course, vanish, either after an adverse decision, or before they even go near a court. Mr Blunkett or Home Secretaries after him, can pass any bills on immigration they like, but they should remember that down the road the British judiciary, lawyers and Strasbourg lie in wait.

Home Secretary Jack Straw said when it was ratified:

> The Universal Declaration makes it clear that it is the duty of states to promote and protect all human rights. Human rights are for everyone to enjoy everywhere ...[4]

Who could possibly object to a law that upheld the rights of people all over the world? But that was precisely the trouble. We had bound ourselves to uphold the freedom not just of British citizens but rights of people everywhere. If a man were persecuted in Afghanistan and could get to Britain, we had to treat him as our own.

It was then that the true nightmare of illegal asylum began. What had been previously a serious problem became intractable. Everybody, including people who have cheated, lied or forged their way into our home, as well as genuine victims of foreign terror, has the keys to our doors. All they have to do when they arrive is to tell the immigration officer that they are victims of political or personal violence in their country of origin. Once they have done so, their chances of being deported are vanishingly small.

They can also claim the right to our welfare and social security funds. These funds, set aside for the old and the sick, are now open to people who have never contributed to them. We have agreed to share our savings with the world. It is a magnet. In 1997 the Conservative government barred refugees who did not declare themselves at the port of entry from applying for social security. The numbers of 'asylum' seekers fell drastically. Below is an extract from the Home Office report on immigration for that year:

> The number of applications for asylum (excluding dependants) received in the UK in 1997 was 32,500, some 2,900 more than in 1996 but 11,500 fewer than in 1995. An important factor in the lower numbers of applications since 1995 was the introduction in February 1996 of DSS benefit restrictions to asylum seekers ...

> The proportion of applications made in-country—that is by people who had already entered the UK in some other capacity—fell from nearly 60 per cent in 1996 to 50 per cent in the last year. In 1997 there was a decrease of 1,300 to 15,900 in the number of in-country applications, and an increase of 4,200 to 16,600 in the number of port applications.[5]

'In-country' applications refer to those migrants who entered as students or tourists but, when discovered, or because they wished to gain access to our social security savings, suddenly 'remembered' they were asylum seekers.

But the courts ruled that barring such asylum seekers from the funds was illegal. Payments resumed and the numbers of asylum seekers rose again. It has continued to rise ever since. As a result Britain, which once colonised the world, is being colonised.

The phrase 'asylum seekers' conjures up a picture of columns of refugees winding their way out of burning cities, of people being tortured in unspeakable prisons. But most are nothing of the sort.

Most are ordinary. Nearly all of them have some money or credit, even if it is only a willingness to work at any job to pay back the cost of getting here. Some are young men who have dropped out of family life and who have come to live in the West. How many become involved in crime is unknown, but the existing figures are worrying.

Police arrests of petty criminals in Hounslow, West London, over a period of four months to April 2002 resulted in 272 immigrants (mainly from Eastern Europe) being sent home. Of the 272 the majority were arrested for carrying out crimes such as shoplifting and similar offences.[6]

Among some 200,000 Russians émigrés now in the UK— one of the fastest growing minorities in the country— organised low-level crime is reported to be growing. A Mafia centered around *Vori v Zakone* ('Thieves in Law') is reported to prey on Russian young men in Britain who do not have proper documents and work in sweatshops.[7]

Few asylum seekers ever go back. Of the 92,000 who arrived in the UK last year, very few, perhaps eight per cent, will leave, and if they do a good proportion will be on air tickets paid for by the British taxpayer. Only a handful will be physically deported.

> I would be surprised if we were removing more than 12 people a month who really don't want to go home. We don't have a working method at the moment for removing people ... the general view of our members is that asylum really has collapsed as a concept.[8]

A huge world-wide people-smuggling industry has grown up to meet this demand. With an estimated turnover of almost £5 billion a year[9]—last year British Airways turned over nearly £9 billion—it offers destinations to all countries. Not only does people-smuggling make money in its own right, but it stokes a new global economy which treats the world as a pool of mobile labour. It is good not only for the people smugglers, but good for global industry. The young Tamil fresh from the back of a truck who serves you at a petrol station on Sunday does not expect to be paid overtime or even normal time: quarter-time is wealth.

> Alongside the proliferation of multinational corporations there has been an equally dramatic growth of the shadow industries—people-smuggling and trafficking—with a massive shadow migration accompanying them. Migrant smuggling is today a comparable 'multinational' enterprise, with competitive global profit levels estimated at USD 5-7 billion a year. People have increasingly become commodities in this trade.[10]

All pockets are catered for. You can fly into London with a set of immaculately forged papers. Alternatively, you can pay a gang to get you to Calais then try to jump a freight train through the Channel Tunnel. You can come by small inflatable and land somewhere on our enormous coastline or you can arrive as a bogus student or tourist and, once you get to Heathrow, announce you are fleeing persecution.

Not everybody uses the smugglers. The well-informed, who can persuade a British Embassy they are going to Britain on a visit and have sufficient funds and a return ticket, can gain entry to Britain legally. Once on British soil they can ask for asylum.

The demand is unquenchable. The mobs of people trying to storm the trains at Calais, the 58 Chinese found dead in a truck in June 2000,[11] the turf wars between smuggling gangs in Kent and France, are signs of the strength of this demand.[12] People will do anything to get here. In May 2002 the press of refugees trying to get through the Channel Tunnel was so great that all freight services to and from Britain had to be suspended.[13]

Migration is welcomed by completely opposite political camps. Enthusiasts of global capital say that, however much pain migration causes now, the market will in time correct its injustices. As people move and labour costs fall, prices will fall world-wide and poverty will recede everywhere. What we are seeing at Dover docks, in Bradford, in cheap Paris tower blocks or in Chinese and Indian sweatshops in New York, is a levelling operation. One day, thanks to international migration, the price of bread from New York to Bangladesh will be the same. Everybody will be able to buy. Capitalism, not communism, is the great leveller.

The antiglobalists see mass migration as a New Jerusalem. They talk of 'deterritorilisation' (sic) and the end of the oppressive nation state. No longer will an accident of birth entitle you to wealth or condemn you to poverty. Migrants may be poor and wretched, but they are the future world citizens. One day everybody will have a right, backed by international law, to settle and work where they like.

Both groups encourage the public to believe that migrants are our economic and social salvation. Every time the subject comes up in the media, the mantra is repeated that without migrants we will not survive economically or socially. There is much talk of preserving our support ratio, that is the number of young people needed to keep the economy going in order to support an increasingly elderly population. If we do not accept migrants, then with our population ageing rapidly and our birthrates falling, Britain will become an understaffed old people's home with no income.

This idea has taken hold with all the force of a religious conviction. Like many religious convictions, it is based on wishful thinking.

Dr David Coleman, Professor of Demography at Oxford University, writes:

> Immigration cannot 'solve' population ageing except at the cost of third-world rates of population growth, for example doubling the population of the EU every 50 years and of course quite quickly displacing the existing population to a minority—'Replacement Migration' indeed.[14]

The danger is that most of the migrants we are now taking are employable only so long as the economy holds up. In a recession we are going to be faced with millions of people on welfare who have made very little, if any, contribution to the country's insurance fund.

The government is paralysed. Terrified of appearing racist, in hock to big business, they resort to news management. At intervals ministers announce on radio and TV new ways of controlling migration. Such announcements are pounced on by a liberal media who fillet them for words like 'flooding' or 'swamped'. When discovered, the minister is duly crucified for being a racist.

In its latest attempt to free itself from the quick sands of illegal migration the Labour government has now started to admit large numbers of legal migrants under a work permit scheme. In 2001 nearly 110,000 were admitted to the country for a stay of up to five years (see figure 3, p. 16). A recent government spending review suggests the government plans to allow a further 175,000 work permit holders into the country next year. There is no evidence that the government makes any serious attempt to check their credentials.

Nearly all will be eligible to remain under existing regulations but, if refused, they could make an appeal under Section 8 of the Human Rights Act guaranteeing a right to family and private life.

This will substantially increase the number of new settlers in the UK, as asylum seekers (China excepted) tend to come from different places from work-permit applicants.[15]

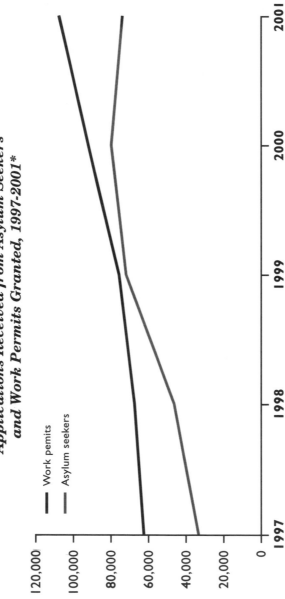

Figure 3
Applications Received from Asylum Seekers
and Work Permits Granted, 1997-2001*

Note: * A change in procedures may have resulted in some under-recording for the fourth quarter of 2000 and the first quarter of 2001.

Source: Mallourides, E. and Turner, G., *Control of Immigration Statistics United Kingdom 2001*, London: Office for National Statistics; Heath, T. and Hill, R., *Asylum Statistics United Kingdom 2001*, the Home Office Research Development and Statistics Directorate (National Statistics), 31 July 2002, figure 1.

3

A brief history of immigration

Defenders of migration say that Britain has always been a mongrel society, and that we should not be concerned about the changes we see. For example, Jonathan Duffy, writing for the BBC in April 2001, stated that 'the notion of racial purity among the British is a fallacy, and our multiculturalism dates back to the Dark Ages and beyond'.[1]

This is nonsense. Before the twentieth century settlement which we are now experiencing, the last great invasion of Britain was that of the Danes in the ninth century. They settled here after the Peace of Wedmore in 875 AD. From then until 1950 Britain remained, save for a few minor incursions, undisturbed. William and the Normans came in 1066, followed by 100,000 Huguenots at the end of the seventeenth century, and 150,000 Jews from the sixteenth to the twentieth centuries. Although their effect was often far greater in proportion to their numbers than those of modern migrants (who can be counted in the millions), their arrival remained, unlike modern migration, an invasion of close cousins. Not even the arrival of large numbers of Irish in the nineteenth and twentieth centuries dented the essential characteristics of the British, a mono-culture dominated by Anglo Saxons, Celts and Iberians.

For Europe, whence Britain almost exclusively drew its peoples, was a continent of genetically linked tribes. Four out of five European males share a Y chromosome belonging to a Palaeolithic ancestor who lived 40,000 years ago.[2] Very few areas of the world were so distinct, and none more so than the island of Britain which for nearly 2,000 years remained as racially separate as Polynesia.[3]

The Newcomers

Things began to change in 1945. Britain, close to destitution, its reserves exhausted by war, was about to lose its empire. Britain fell back on the idea of the Commonwealth, a free association of nations from the Empire it had founded in 1931. In 1948 the Labour Government passed the British Nationality Act. This gave eight hundred million Commonwealth citizens the legal right to reside in the United Kingdom.

When Churchill came to power he was strongly opposed to immigration, but bureaucratic drift and a lack of policy led to its increase. Under his administration, immigration rose from 3,000 in 1953 to 42,650 in 1955. After Churchill, the numbers steadied, fell, then rose again to 136,400 in 1961.[4]

Few at the time gave much thought to the consequences. But they were immediate. Andrew Roberts wrote in *Eminent Churchillians*:

> The New Commonwealth immigrants on the other hand arrived at a period of full employment and took largely blue collar jobs which would have been done by the indigenous population or phased out altogether by labour saving devices. One of the unquantifiable by-products of immigration is the extent to which cheap labour slowed up the drive for greater productivity in British industry, to the long-term detriment of the entire economy. At a time when Britain desperately needed to move from labour- to capital-intensive structures, immigration held her back.[5]

It was not just economics. Ordinary people hated and resented the newcomers. From about 1954, Enoch Powell reported that Commonwealth immigration was the principal and, at times, the only political issue in Wolverhampton South West.[6] A divide was opening between the government and the governed which, as Andrew Roberts remarked, 'helped break the habit of social deference within the Conservative party and end the long domination of the upper and middle classes'.[7]

For race, like much else in Britain until the eighties, was a class matter. Those in the official classes, especially High Tories and Liberal Socialists, thought of themselves as being 'good at dealing with the natives', especially in comparison with America. The US had race riots, lynchings and white mob law. At least when it came to race, the British could show the Americans how centuries of imperial rule paid off.

However, immigration remained deeply unpopular with ordinary British people. In 1948 the ex-troopship Empire Windrush docked in Tilbury carrying 492 West Indian migrants. Many of them were ex-servicemen who wanted to return to a Britain they had served in during the war. All were, under the immigration laws of the day, entitled to settle here. They were not welcomed. Two days after the ship docked, eleven Labour MPs wrote to Prime Minister Clement Atlee complaining that: 'An influx of coloured people domiciled here is likely to impair the harmony, strength and cohesion of our public and social life.'8 People refused them accommodation and the government had to house half of them in a deep air raid shelter on Clapham Common.

It was a great shock. They were hard working, God-fearing people with strong lower middle-class values. In the colonies they had been taught that Britain was one great family of equal peoples. They never got over their disappointment at being rejected. One old man said: 'I used to go to bed at night hoping to wake up white.'9

They were followed by a wave of Bangladeshi and Indian immigration. Part of that influx has always been attributed by the Left to Enoch Powell.10 It is widely believed that, as Conservative Health Minister from 1960 to 1964, he urged his cabinet colleagues that immigration from the black commonwealth should be encouraged in order to combat a shortage of doctors and nurses.

But Powell always denied this. He claimed that as Health Minister he had no power over the entry of doctors or nurses to Britain. This, he said, was in the gift of the General Medical Council and the General Nursing Council. Powell was later to accuse the General Medical Council of a betrayal of standards by allowing large numbers of Indian doctors into the country.11 In the year he left office, 360 New

Commonwealth doctors entered Britain with qualifications accepted by the GMC. By 1973 the yearly intake was 3,000.[12]

Britain in the 1960s was not an easy place to settle. It was a country in which slight differences in the way you pronounced the letter 'r' labelled you servant or master. In a rigidly traditional society, the sudden arrival of West Indians and, soon after, Indians and Pakistanis, provoked muted hysteria. 'No Pakis or Coloureds' went up in landladies' windows.

As the numbers became large, Enoch Powell began to forecast an apocalypse. A formidable classical scholar who had once dreamed of becoming Viceroy of India, he saw in the arrival of huge numbers of people from across an even more distant Rhine, the Indus, strong parallels with the fall of Rome.

Europe, like ancient Rome, would become a victim of its own success. Just as migration, much of it by slaves, had filled ancient Rome from the impossibly distant lands of Hungary, Ireland, Scotland and Ukraine, so modern migration, Powell felt, would fill Europe with alien faces.

The same mechanisms were at work then as they are now. An efficient transport system brought impoverished people to Rome from all over the Empire. A network of posting roads meant it was possible to get from Rome to central France in a week, or, by rowing galley, from Athens in ten days, or Alexandria in three weeks. For the times, these were Concorde-like speeds. The world began to move.

The first to come were wealthy foreigners, bringing their slaves. More slaves came as people, hearing of Rome's wealth, sold themselves for transportation. For although slaves were taken in victory, in those days many people sold their freedom as they might sell their land. It was often worth more. Many slaves were frequently treated well or even better than poor freemen. Some even reached the councils of the Emperor. After some years a slave could purchase his freedom.

But in Rome's last years migrants arrived to find a declining power in desperate need of slaves, servants and labour to support a patrician class which refused to send its sons into the army to defend Rome's frontiers, which avoided taxes, and used the mob to pressure public opinion. But the Imperial City had one thing still to sell: Roman citizenship. It began to grant the once precious honour to those who would serve in its legions, or to frontier towns who would hold the line against the enemy. As Carcopino wrote in *Daily Life in Ancient Rome*:

> Where previously only the most exalted of foreigners were granted citizenship, naturalisations were extended at one stroke either to a class of demobilised auxiliaries or to a municipality suddenly converted into an honorary colony.[13]

Whole legions consisted of Romanised tribes who fought for the Empire one day then made accommodations with the enemy the next. *Pugnabuntne milites*? ('Will the legions fight?') became a commonplace question. By 476 AD Odacer, the German general in charge of the Roman Army in North Italy, deposed the last Western Emperor and handed Europe over to 600 years of barbarian rule. The Eastern Empire survived, but for the Western Empire civilisation was extinguished. By the sixth century Rome and the surrounding *campagna* had become a hunting ground for the Lombards, who, raiding from the North, picked over the inhabitants as they might cattle.

'The inhabitants of Rome,' wrote Gibbon in *The Decline and Fall of the Roman Empire*, '...beheld from the walls the flames of their houses and heard the lamentations of their brethren, who were coupled together like dogs and dragged away into distant slavery beyond the seas and the mountains...' The hub of the world descended into decay.

On 20 April 1968, Powell looked into Britain's future and saw the same vision. Quoting Virgil he declared: 'As I look ahead, I am filled with foreboding. Like the Roman I seem to see the river Tiber foaming with much blood.' Britain, he said, was 'busily engaged in heaping up its own funeral pyre'. The then Labour government was 'literally mad' to allow large-scale immigration.[14]

Powell was fired from the shadow cabinet by Edward Heath, but such was the popularity of his remarks, he not only retained his seat with a huge majority but caused a Tory swing in nearby constituencies, resulting in the return of Heath to power. He was not rewarded with a Cabinet post.

The Left denounced him as a fascist, a hater of the poor, the weak and the crippled, a second Hitler. But the Right enthused over this prophet come to judgement. 'Enoch was right' became a secret invocation to the old British way of life. Racism was not concealed. It was common for black men strolling in the street to be taunted with shouts of 'Nigger go home'.

The government decided that the best way to deal with coloured migration was to legislate it out of existence. The Race Relations Act of 1965, which created the offence of incitement to racial hatred and made discrimination illegal in public places, was followed by a new act in 1968 prohibiting discrimination in respect of goods, services, facilities, employment and accommodation. A further Act in 1976 prohibited indirect racial discrimination. The state had effectively legislated for compulsory colour-blindness. It became illegal to notice that people were from different races, to draw attention to a person's colour or to base any sort of judgment on the basis of their race.

It is a paradox that Powell, a stark, forbidding figure with an English weakness for self-caricature, was the midwife to the modern liberal desire for as much migration as possible. He alerted the Left to the possibility that the social order in Britain could be effectively swept away by encouraging as many migrants as possible to enter the country. Migrants, a new army of the poor, would, unlike the stubbornly right-wing British white working class, wake Britain from its class-filled slumbers. Owing no loyalty to our oppressive institutions, it would overthrow the rule of old, greedy white men like Powell.

A Powellite demonology began to be constructed. The left-wing magazine *Searchlight* related how, when Powell dined with a journalist who 'suggested that it might be charitable for Powell, as a Christian, at least to ask his supporters to be good neighbours to those black people already in Britain

... Powell did not respond but just carried on tucking into his lunch'.[15]

Powell's views, the Left decided, must never be heard again. For the remainder of the century all debate on immigration was stifled. A rigorous internal self-censorship on race, religious in its intensity, fell over the country. To criticise migration was to be labelled a Nazi, and a supporter of the holocaust. The holocaust itself became a pivotal study in schools. This was what white people were capable of. Thinking about another person's colour was to take the first step back down the road to Belsen and the Einsatz Kommando. The new religion was not Christianity but equality. Its mortal sin was racism.

But, despite Powellism, and the 'racism' of the British, people came. They still do. New Rome, London in 2002, offers the same pull on the imaginations of millions of people of all colours. Here is a land you can see at the press of a TV button, a dream country in which the streets are clean, the police unarmed, the judges honest, a country that can be reached on one of the huge jets that batter the sky over the slums of the city you live in. The price of a ticket on one of these jets falls every year. An Indian family would have to work for five years in the 1960s to earn enough for one of them to go to London. Today the same ticket can be bought with six months' wages.

With cheap air travel, the number of migrants has increased. In 1979, 5,000 people asked for asylum in the UK. Most were from India and Pakistan. But, by the middle of the 1980s, an immigration officer recalls, so many migrants were arriving from the Indian subcontinent that hundreds were sleeping on the floor of the holding area at Heathrow waiting to be let in. Visas were introduced, but like a tap to be turned on and off as demand and political pressure varied. They marked the death knell of the wholly unrealistic idea of a commonwealth whose citizens were free to come and go as they pleased.

But if you could not knock at the door, you could still climb through a side window. People-smuggling began. It was small-scale at first, but by the early nineties large numbers of Eastern Europeans were joining the flow. These were added to later by refugees from the Balkan war, the war against Iraq and—a new phenomenon—the arrival of large numbers of Chinese. People-smuggling began to be taken over by organised crime. Not only was it profitable, but it had the advantage that it could be run in conjunction with prostitution, child slavery and drug running. Many came via Scandinavia. The following report tells of a young woman lured by the traffickers with promises of a better life in Europe or America:

> The language around her incomprehensible, her passport taken from her by the man she now recognised as a pimp, she started sobbing. 'I don't want to do that!' 'If you don't do it I can lock you up in the apartment and have customers come over,' he shouted back. 'What did you expect? You are a young girl going to another country.'[16]

Traditional gangs known as the Snakeheads linked up with the Russian Mafia to throw a bridge into Europe. Not only Chinese were exported. Migrants from Sri Lanka, India and Pakistan began to be ferried through a Moscow hub to London. Others came via the Mediterranean. Some made the long overland journey by road from Afghanistan. Some paid fantastic sums in the equivalent local currency.

> The situation was very bad in Afghanistan. Every day the Taliban came to take me or things from our house. It was very dangerous for me so the decision was to send me out to save my life. I was very heavy because my life was in danger. It was the first time I was separated from my father or my mother. I had very hard feelings. We sold our house and our shop and the things in it for $10,000. We sold all. It took 20 days walking, then sometimes in lorries, sometimes with a lot of people, sometimes with a few. Sometimes we stayed seven days without food, sometimes ten. I feel very happy to be away from the dangers in my country.
>
> (Ahmed, 16 years old, Dover hostel) [17]

A Tamil explained how he came here. His family paid the uncles £6,000. He took a plane to Bangkok and from there to Algeria. There he said he met ten other people. They waited for many days in a small place by a beach before a boat came and took them out to sea for three days. One morning they woke to see that they were at another beach.

The men on the boat put them ashore and then left. They waited and waited and then they saw an Indian man coming. The Tamil was very angry as he thought they had been tricked and he was in India. But the man was not an Indian but an Italian. They were in Italy. 'I am lonely here in London. I send a lot of my money home. Soon I will be sent a wife.' Did he draw the dole? 'Yes.' But he is working? He was puzzled by the question. 'Of course I am working.'[18]

By 2001, 71,365 heads of families (6,000 a month) were asking for asylum at our ports. If family members are included, then the figure rises to 92,000.[19] In addition, 76,700 husbands, wives and children of settled migrants and other residents arrived.[20] We do not know how many slipped into the country illegally, but most migration experts believe that 80 per cent of asylum seekers declare themselves, so we might add another 15 per cent—13,800—making the above total 105,000. But it could be even higher.

Of the asylum seekers, we can expect around 12 per cent to be removed, leaving 93,104. Some 10 per cent will be granted asylum, around 17 per cent will be given exceptional leave to remain, and the rest will disappear.

Such an influx has changed Britain. Islam is our fastest growing religion. Leicester is projected to be the first city in which whites will be in a minority. London and two or three of our major cities are expected to follow by 2020. In fact, so great is the influx of immigrants that London is absorbing a city the size of Leeds every three or four years.

4

How to get in

By no means all people come in the back of trucks. The simplest way of entering Britain is to obtain a tourist or student visa from a local British Embassy and fly to London. Eighty-seven million people enter into Britain each year, a quarter of them tourists. Most, of course, are what they say they are. But some have come to stay. If you have a visa, and can show you have sufficient funds, the immigration officer will stamp your passport with permission to remain for three to six months.

You walk out of the airport and take a bus. You are in your new country. In a few months time, when you have settled in and see if you like it or not, you can ask for asylum. You are not required to ask for asylum as soon as you enter. Some do, but it is wiser to get the feel of the place before you take on the authorities. You will find plenty of friends in the country who have been through the process.

If you come as a student, the same thing applies. Student visas are easy to obtain, many low-grade universities and colleges are regarded by smugglers as little more than entry visa processing offices.[1] To remain funded they need students. It is believed that thousands of illegal settlers arrive in the UK via the 'student' route each year.

Chinese gangs provide false diplomas to Chinese who want to go to England as students for more education. The number of Chinese students accepted by British universities increased from 56 in 1996 to 1,462 in 2000—the total number of foreign students rose from 27,518 to 31,029. The gangs not only provide a diploma that certifies a high school or college application, but also fill out university application forms, write reference letters and take the English language test. Bank statements showing sufficient funds for foreign study can be 'rented' by applicants for student visas.[2]

One country which is exceptionally vulnerable to this influx of 'students' is Ireland. It has open borders with the UK.

Chinese Triad gang members are enrolling in Dublin language schools. Under unique arrangements with China, Chinese English-language students in Ireland are allowed to work up to 20 hours a week, a privilege denied to other foreign students. Dublin's Chinese population more than doubled in the past two years, to 30,000, and more than half are students. Ireland issued a record 9,000 foreign-student visas in 2000.[3]

The most notorious case of a 'student' entering Britain is that of Valentine Strasser, 'The Butcher of Sierra Leone'. In 1992 Strasser, then aged 26, led a coup in that country in which his troops, according to *The Times*, 'over the next four years murdered, burnt villages and chopped off the hands of countless men, women and children'. Toppled from power in 1996, but supported by the UN who paid for his A-level studies, he entered Britain on a student visa in 1996 and enrolled at a law course at Warwick University. He dropped out and was later discovered by the press in Croydon living on social security but driving a series 7S Mercedes.[4] He has since left, having been denied asylum, but had it not been for huge press publicity it is likely he might still be here.

Work for either the 'student' or the 'tourist' is the next step. It is not difficult to find work as a cleaner or an au pair, but for more interesting or better-paid work you need papers. Without papers you are condemned to the tender mercies of sweat-shop owners and predatory middle-class Britons. Try living outside the state, cleaning private houses, working as a casual builder, or gardening for cash. Suddenly all the brave liberal talk about representation and the need for migrants to be accepted evaporates when it comes to giving notice, or paying wages while an employee is sick. Few middle-class Britons give much thought to why pizzas and curry are so cheap or why the young man in the local petrol station never seems to have any time off.

An Inland Revenue official admitted that the black economy was no longer on the edge of our economy but central to it. Catering, which relies heavily on illegal immigration, makes more money than shipbuilding and coal.[5]

Sophisticated certificate factories now operate in many cities producing high grade forgeries of birth certificates, marriage certificates and other papers that are difficult to tell from the real thing. It may explain why there are increasing numbers of Nigerians called Smith or Macintosh walking the streets. However, it needs a criminal mind and criminal contacts to approach such gangs. The danger is that, once you contact them, they will have you in their power.

The Family... And Marrying Into It

Settlement in Britain brings wives, husbands and children from overseas to join the settler. Figure 4 (p. 31) gives an idea of the scale. Of course, not all of these are coming to join asylum seekers. Many other people in the country bring in family members: work permit holders, people who have lived here all their lives and arrange a marriage abroad, and some who marry abroad and bring their wives or husbands back with them. Children also come to join families.

Marriage is a route to settlement and ultimately citizenship. Once you are married to a British national you can become a citizen. In 2001, 8,855 husbands and 610 male fiancés were admitted for a probationary year prior to settlement. In the same year 17,860 wives and 1,775 fiancées were admitted for a probationary year prior to settlement.[6]

Arranged marriages are a feature of many cultures. Described as traditional, such marriages are completely legal, and result, unless there is outright fraud, in acceptance for settlement.

Those involved deny any sort of coercion, but there have been criticisms of some arranged marriages because they can be vehicles for avoiding immigration controls. In the 1980s, the government tried to prevent this by imposing the primary purpose rule. Its aim was to stop men, especially from the Indian subcontinent, using arranged marriages as a means of obtaining British residence. In 1983 the burden of proving that such a marriage was not one of convenience was placed on the applicant. Labour scrapped the primary purpose rule in 1999. 'In 1999 the number of admissions of wives, husbands and fiancé(e)s from all countries rose to 30,000 compared to 21,000 in 1996, an increase of 50 per cent.'[7]

There have been allegations that some arranged marriages are coercive. School staff in certain parts of Britain have complained of young girls suddenly vanishing from school to return some weeks later having been married to grooms they had never met, and in some cases violently objected to. Those who try to run away, it is alleged, can meet with violence. Some, it is claimed, have been murdered. Local Asian taxi drivers acting as a type of unofficial police force to track down runaways have been reported.[8] This is an area from which the politically correct flee, fearing accusations of racism if they speak out for their less privileged sisters.

No such squeamishness influenced Labour Home Secretary David Blunkett. In early 2002, discussing the use of arranged marriages to avoid immigration control, he spoke of fraudulent marriages being an increasing problem and of forced marriages which abused women's rights. He urged Asians to try and marry within Britain.[9]

Liberal opinion was outraged. Blunkett was condemned by human rights lawyer Sha Sood who said the Home Secretary was imposing his views on Asian communities, and had failed to make a distinction between arranged and forced marriages. There were calls for the Home Secretary to be arraigned for abuses of human rights. Dr Siddiqui, the head of the Muslim parliament, accused Mr Blunkett of using 'racist language'.

But Jagdessh Sing of the Sikh Community Action Network said many marriages involved coercion: 'It is a serious issue within the Asian rank and file in this country. It should not be hidden behind a barrier of cultural distinction and diversity.'

Ann Cryer, Labour MP for Keighley, said on the BBC 'Today' programme: 'Asian girls who are brought in as wives are frequently abandoned by their husbands and in-laws, the people who arranged the marriage don't want to know.'[10]

Yasmin Alibhai Brown, well known for her spirited defence of racial minorities, talked of being incredulous at the attacks mounted on people like Ann Cryer. Writing about abuse (including forced marriage) within Asian families, she said Ann Cryer was 'much admired by young Asian women who no longer feel safe to sit tight and bear it all'.[11]

The police were initially reluctant to act because of racial sensitivities. It took black women's groups to highlight the problem.[12] But, in 2001, women's groups thought there might be 1,000 forced marriages a year, with many going undetected.[13] The Foreign Office receives reports of 200 cases a year, and admits that: 'many go unreported'.[14] Given the understandable reluctance of anybody to report members of their family to the police, these reported cases can only be the most serious. Identifying them does nothing to address the 'grey area' between forced and arranged marriages. We cannot know how many cases of 'obliged' rather than forced marriages there are. Like all forms of domestic abuse, they will, unless the asylum laws are changed, remain hidden.

Wedding Bells as a Career Choice

Unrelated to arranged marriages are multiple marriage rackets. Bigamous marriages, some on an industrial scale, are entered into. Susan Coates, reported *The Times*, married seven West African men within a year, charging £2,500 a time. Her crime was only discovered when a drug dealer was shot outside her flat. (One of her husbands married twice, thinking it would help him with his asylum application.) After her conviction PC Ross Ellison said: 'There is no doubt this was a very well organised marriage scam. It was the sheer simplicity of it, together with the lack of any central cross referencing to show Coates was becoming a bride again and again, that allowed this to go on.'[15]

31

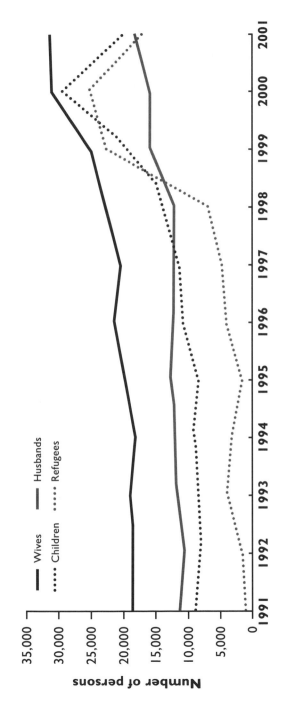

Figure 4
Grants of Settlement of Spouses, Children and Refugees, 1991-2001

Source: Mallourides, E. and Turner, G., *Control of Immigration: Statistics United Kingdom, 2001*, 26 September 2002, p. 11.

5

How to stay

While brides and close relatives have little problem in establishing residence, the life of a clandestine settler is more difficult. It is not easy to live outside the tax and benefit system and there is the constant fear of discovery. It is much better to wait until all legal avenues of appeal are exhausted and then go illegal, rather than the other way around.

This is why it is believed that the majority of illegal settlers (80 per cent) ask for asylum. Very few asylum seekers are ever thrown out, and while you are awaiting a decision by the Home Office you can work illegally and draw various benefits. Gangs do not pay benefits, the British government does. Gangs do not pay for a lawyer. The British government will. The key is the Human Rights Act, which Britain obeys to the letter.

When an immigration officer asks an asylum seeker for his story, one of the things he is trying to find out is if his rights under the Act have been violated. If they have, the officer is obliged to admit him so that a court can test his application for citizenship. The test is not of the suitability of the individual. Drug barons who fear reprisals from their fellow criminals in Colombia have been given leave to remain under the terms of the Human Rights Act. Had Hitler come to Britain in April 1944, having fled a Nazi coup against him, and had the Act been in force, he would have been entitled to asylum. We cannot send anybody, however vile, back to a country where his or her individual rights will be violated.

Once your asylum request is lodged, you are free to enter Britain while your case is being considered by the Home Office. If they refuse to accept your story—and it may take months or even years (less likely recently) before they get around to considering it—you can appeal. You are not supposed to work. It is, however, easy to do so in Britain's thriving black economy.

These rules apply even if an asylum seeker has already passed through two or three European countries which have signed the Act. One might think that a genuine asylum seeker would be grateful to get to the first country that could offer him asylum and stay there, but that is often not the case.

Had Britain signed the Schengen Agreement, which created a Europe without internal frontiers in 1999, we could send such 'cherry pickers' back to France or the first EU country they came to. Sangatte would not have existed. We declined to sign the treaty because of fears of terrorism, our 'special geographical position' and 'traditional links' with the Commonwealth. These arguments are mendacious. When it comes to modern immigration control, 'traditional links' count for nothing. In a world of international jet travel, the Channel Tunnel and super-ferries, island Britain, approached by four steam ferries a day, has long gone.

Defenders of our failure to sign the Schengen agreement say that another treaty, the Dublin Convention, protects us from what are known as 'forum shopping' asylum seekers, looking for the country with the most benefits. Under the Dublin Convention, refugees were supposed to apply for asylum in the first EU country they arrived in. But this convention has been turned on its head. A recent Home Office document advises lawyers and immigration officials that the convention must give precedence to ensuring that refugees on arrival in the EU are reunited with their families.[1] A lower priority is given to ensuring that asylum seekers ask for asylum in the first EU country they come to.

The immigration officer knows he cannot send you back to France. We used to have an agreement with France to send people back, but the Labour government tore it up in 1997.[2] Moreover, in 2000 the Law Lords ruled France an unsafe country to return migrants to.[3] The French have too tough a policy on repatriating migrants.

Nor is there a 'white list' of safe countries refugees can be sent to. It was scrapped a few years ago under pressure from immigration lobbies. Labour, although it furiously opposed it in opposition, now wants to bring it back. Labour also wants to be able to send people back to their own countries to await an appeal, if those countries are safe and their claims are clearly unfounded.

These proposals are likely—as many before them—to run into the quick sands of the Human Rights Act. Courts are likely to make hay with the phrase 'clearly unfounded'. A parliamentary committee reported in June 2002 that Home Secretary David Blunkett's asylum reforms might contain up to 14 breaches of human rights.[4] The committee suggested that even those people whose claims for asylum were manifestly unfounded could not be removed before they had a hearing in a British court. They also felt that stopping social security for those who have been asked to leave asylum centres was an abuse, as was separate education of the children of asylum seekers.

The process of endless appeals, judicial reviews and adjournments will continue—all to the great benefit of the legal profession.

The immigration officer will have these laws (or lack of them) in his mind as he studies your documents. Unless you are on a wanted list of known war criminals or terrorists, his powers are nil. He will know that virtually all those cases he has detained have been freed, and of the next 100 cases he will give temporary leave to remain this year, probably none will ever go home. The independent think tank MigrationwatchUK reports:

In Germany three per cent of applicants are granted asylum; in Britain 30 per cent are granted asylum or its close equivalent, exceptional leave to remain (ELR). In France the chance of an Algerian receiving asylum is five per cent, in Britain it is 80 per cent.

Even if the application fails there is no effective removal system. The process of decision making takes so long applicants can, and do, disappear into their own communities, often in city centres. Thereafter they can live without documentation and can benefit from free health, education and housing. In Germany and

France, for example, police carry out sweeps, examining documents and deporting immigrants.[5]

Meanwhile the invisible flow of migrants into Britain in the form of bogus students and tourists, at least as great if not greater than those who hide themselves in trucks or present themselves to the immigration officers at Dover, will continue.

If the immigration officer grants you temporary leave to enter, he will hand you some forms and direct you to an official who will take you from the airport to a hotel. There you will be given some money by a government sponsored charity, and directions on how to reach the nearest immigration office, usually in London. You are free to go. At the immigration office you will learn that you are entitled to various social security benefits.

Within a few weeks you will get a letter from the Home Office. Usually it will tell you that your application to remain in Britain has been considered but that it has been refused. You will be given a date to leave the country. You can then appeal against the decision to a tribunal.

But even if an applicant for asylum is refused, it is not hopeless. Appeals can be spun out for years, your lawyer can ask for a judicial review, you might marry in the interim (having children is a powerful argument for the courts allowing you to stay) or, if the worst comes to the worst, you can buy a new identity and simply disappear. Or you can sit tight and wait for deportation. In many cases, the Home Office will forget about you (their records are in chaos), or they will issue you with a notice to leave and offer you a ticket home. This is classed in their records as a deportation. Only rarely, and only if you present yourself as a sitting duck, will they come and physically drag you to the airport. At £38,000 a deportation costs too much.

It is over deportation that recent government proposals to send back asylum seekers within days of their arrival are likely to run into the ground. Deportations are extraordinarily expensive, there are many countries who will not take asylum seekers back and asylum seekers often refuse to say where they come from. 'I do not know' is not a country that issues passports.

Large-scale deportations also face the enormous political risk of somebody being killed. Joy Gardner, a Jamaican woman, died when police and immigration officers tried to forcibly remove her from her home and deport her. Riots followed her death. This tragedy has been kept alive by various anti-racist groups. The following alleged account on the internet by the Socialist Equality Party gives a flavour of the politics:

> Joy, a 40 year old Jamaican mother of two, came to Britain legally (sic) from Jamaica in 1987 to be reunited with her mother and family. She applied for leave to stay on compassionate grounds. Joy's appeal was rejected without her being informed, and deportation procedures instigated against her and her five-year-old son, Graeme. At 7.40 in the morning, five police officers and an immigration official forced their way into her home. Joy was thrown to the ground, bound with leather belts and gagged with 13 feet of surgical tape. She suffocated, suffering massive brain damage and never regained consciousness. On August 1, 1993 her life support was ended.[6]

No British government is going to put a match to such a powder keg. Few police or immigration officers are likely to want to co-operate in an activity that might cost them their careers and possibly land them in jail. When it comes to race, the government will not back you. David Blunkett has made his own fears on this apparent in a recent reply in the House of Commons:

> ...we do not wish to tear neighbourhoods, communities and different ethnic cultures apart in the process [of deportation]. Otherwise, we could send the police out en masse, collect people, stick them on planes and send them away; there has to be a balance. If I can get 100 per cent of those who should not be here through the new system and out of the country, I will, but I would welcome a bit more sensitivity and help from people such as the hon. gentleman.[7]

Blunkett's statement did not stop banner headlines announcing a target of 30,000 removals a year. Like almost all government promises on migration, this was soon toned down. On 31 August 2002, Beverley Hughes, the government's immigration minister, announced a more 'achievable' deportation target to be set later that year:

The 30,000 target that was set some time ago wasn't really a target that, within the capacity of the organisation at that time, was readily achievable... We need to look again at the target.[8]

She did not put a number on it. Last year the government only persuaded 10,000 to go, almost all of them voluntarily, many of whom had their fares paid.[9] Meanwhile, each year between 50,000 and 60,000 asylum seekers, who have had their applications to stay refused, slip quietly into society.

6

The tribunals

Unlike France, where asylum seekers are brought before a judge within four days,[1] and if your case is rejected matters move briskly, in Britain it may be years before immigration officers come knocking on your door, if ever.

Asylum seekers in Britain refused leave to remain by the Home Office can appeal to an immigration appeals tribunal. It can take between six months and a year before your case is heard. It used to be much longer, but it is now getting quicker since strong public disapproval of asylum seeking began to make itself felt. Asylum tribunals have the same status as a full sitting of a county court. These are real courts, not 'trestle-table' justice with bureaucrats shuffling papers of deportees. They are British justice in full fig.

The proceedings are adversarial. The refugee is represented by a barrister. The Home Office can send a presenting officer or counsel to oppose the refugee's application if they wish. The adjudicator is in effect a judge, presiding over a court that has the same powers to summon witnesses and decide on evidence as any other court. Its judgements are minutely scrutinised by the higher courts.

But there are flaws in this system. It is difficult to:

1. Verify the evidence presented by the appellant

2. Challenge expert witness statements brought by the defence.

These difficulties are compounded by Home Office and defence solicitors often being inexperienced or badly prepared. Statements are made about the conditions in the country the appellant comes from, and the mental or physical state of the appellant, which often seem doubtful. All the expert witnesses seem to be on one side—that of the appellant.

Figure 5
**Appeals Determined by IAA Adjudicators
Quarter 4 1999 - Quarter 3 2002**

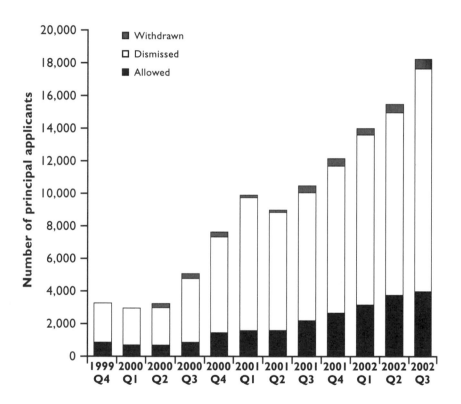

Source: *Home Office Statistics: 4th Quarter 2001, UK*, 14 March 2002, p. 5, and
   Asylum Statistics: 3rd Quarter 2002, UK, Home Office, 29 November
   2002, p. 5.

The following cases are accounts of appeals made by
asylum seekers at tribunals in the Greater London area
between 2001 and 2002. With the exception of the case
'Raped in the Congo', which was witnessed by a third party,
the writer attended each hearing.

Second time around

Some cases appear bogus from the outset, especially where evidence of wrongdoing within the UK is discovered. A young Kosovan man with a shaven head appears at a tribunal flanked by two lawyers from a charity. He says he is a gypsy. If he returns to Kosovo he will be killed.

The Home Office barrister intervenes to tell the court that this man was picked up by the police on an unrelated matter. Only after a routine fingerprint check was made was it discovered he had made more than one application for asylum and had been deported the previous year. Now, a few months later, here he was back in the country. The lawyers from the charity, completely unaware of this, are forced to withdraw.

Nobody knows if he is a gypsy or not. Nor can he produce any evidence that the area he came from is badly policed by the international police force in Kosovo. Nor is he able to explain exactly who—except in the most general terms—he is frightened of. Local villagers, gangs, people he owes money to, or is he a genuine gypsy in fear of his life? However, he does appear to be genuinely frightened of something. He is unlikely to succeed in his appeal.

A normal society like this

A young man, a Serb, handsome, tall, but ill-at-ease, sits in an asylum appeals court in London. He is about 30 with an intelligent face. Sitting on his right is a translator. Facing the adjudicator of the court is a lawyer. From the latter's beautifully cut suit to his discreet gold buckled loafers, he looks expensive. He is there to present the case for the appellant. The adjudicator sits under the Royal Coat of Arms on the bench. Now and again the door opens to admit a clerk who bows to the coat of arms. An empty chair stands next to the expensive lawyer. This is the seat for the Home Office representative. They have not bothered to send anybody to try and stop this man settling here.

The appellant, an ethnic Serb, fled via Austria to France in 1996. The French refused him asylum and he came to England. He once lived in Croatia. He has been refused asylum here by the Home Office. He is now appealing. He is asked what will happen to him should he go back to Croatia. He would be questioned by the police as to why he was in England. He moistens his lips and says, 'A lot of violence.'

He cannot say what would happen to him, only what has happened to friends. They were questioned and interrogated by the police, beaten up and obliged to report every seven days. How would people know he was a Serb? 'There is a special mark on the passport so Croatian police always know you are a Serb.'

Does he know any people who were harmed? He mentions a name and shifts uneasily in his seat: 'He was detained in Zagreb for several days and when he was released, detained in a police station in Vukovar and then beaten up.'

Why did he not consider settling in Serbia? 'The authorities were very autocratic and refugees were mobilised for fighting in Kosovo.' Why did he not claim asylum in Greece? 'I thought things would never go back to the way they were.'

He says his girlfriend is expecting a baby. 'I want it to grow up in a normal society like this.' He begins to cry very quietly, recovers and falls silent. His lawyer puts in his plea, proffers some more papers in evidence, reports on conditions in the Balkans, precedents are passed back and forth between the bench and the lawyer, then as abruptly as it began, the case finishes.

If the young man is refused, with a baby coming things will be hard. What he wanted, in effect, was permission to join the tax and full benefit system. If you get permission to stay you can go on drawing social security until you get a job when you can go on PAYE. If not, it is possible to go underground, perhaps getting a job as a waiter for a restaurant owner who is himself an illegal, but at terrible wages, perhaps a couple of pounds an hour, with no holidays and lots of abuse.

Yet the court has almost nothing to go on in this case. It is true that a fragmented Yugoslavia is a dangerous place (much less so than it was), but compared with what? The slums of Chicago are probably more dangerous. So are American prisons. The US practices capital punishment.

Prisoners not subject to the death penalty can be condemned to multiple life sentences. In some states released prisoners are denied the vote and some are barred from reasonable work.[2] Each of these laws violates human rights as defined by the Human Rights Act. But we do not see many American refugees in Britain, and it is doubtful that the courts would see it as our job to remedy the American justice system by allowing refugees from the US to claim asylum here.

Raped in the Congo

A black woman in her middle thirties sits in an asylum appeal court. She is from the Democratic Republic of the Congo. Her husband was a supporter of the deposed tyrant Laurent Kabilla. When he was deposed, she was captured by the troops of the 'liberating' army and raped in front of her nine-year-old daughter. Her fingertips tremble as she tells her story to the silent courtroom. Here among white strangers her shame is revealed. Some of the black staff listening will know about Africa with road blocks manned by gun-toting 15-year-olds intent on rape and murder, sleek delegations arriving at the airports, and long Mercedes roaring in and out of the ruler's palace. If she goes back, she says, she will die.

The Home Office wants her deported because it says the Democratic Republic of the Congo has signed the UN convention against torture. The court will probably allow her appeal. But such a decision must be a guess, based on feelings of decency rather than law or fact.

Charged with being a Rwandan

A young woman from the Congo tells the court she was wrongly quoted at her first interview with immigration officials. Her statement was not read back to her or explained. She is asked if she has read the statement since. She says no. 'So how', asks a lawyer, 'do you know it is inaccurate?' A friend read it and told her. The lawyer asks if she is aware of its contents now. 'Yes.' 'Any particular items you are contesting?' 'Right now I cannot say but if you read it back I can say.' Her lawyer goes over her story with her bit by bit. She is then cross-examined by the Home Office lawyer.

She was, she says, arrested in the Congo with her father in 1998. They were Rwandans, held in jail while she was pregnant, deprived of sleep, beaten with a rifle butt and sexually harassed. Eventually her father managed to bribe the guards to let her out. How did her father manage to pay? He was arrested soon after her and must have had some money in his pocket.

She was rearrested in 1999 when she was again pregnant, taken before a tribunal and 'charged' with being a Rwandan. She was acquitted but told to leave the Congo. Her father had to pay another bribe to get her out of jail. She stayed on after her release for another two years. Was it for financial considerations? No, she thought things would get better. How did she eventually leave the country? Her father, who was a businessman, sent an agent to her to help her arrange it. How did she get here? She flew to Belgium, stopped overnight then flew on to Britain. Why did she not claim asylum in Belgium? A lawyer said she could claim asylum in the country of her choice. Asked where her father is now she says he is still in the Congo. She does not know if he has any problems as she is not in contact with him.

Her story seems vague and inconsistent. Two years seems a very long time to wait to flee. Why she challenged the statement at the start is puzzling. One is left wondering if this could be the basis for a fresh appeal if this one goes wrong, or just a feeling of being generally wronged.

'My father was killed by the man who appears in my mirror all the time'

The same uncertainty applies to expert evidence. Cases seem poorly researched, and expert testimony on the political situation in a country, the quality of its refugee or social services, or medical evidence which might be in dispute, is often not presented by both sides.

A badly dressed middle-aged Albanian Kosovan appears at a tribunal. He protests that although he has a serious medical condition brought on by the war in Kosovo, he has been sent by the Home Office to live in the north of England, where he can no longer see his neurologist, or a London GP familiar with his case.

The Home Office claims that he is not a genuine refugee. When he arrived he did not even know the name of the leader of the Kosovan Liberation Army and told immigration officials that the town he came from was in a different province to the one it actually is in.

He claims that these mistakes are the fault of the Home Office. If he were to return he would be in danger of his life. He is also claiming residence in Britain under Section 8 of the European Convention on Human Rights, which guarantees a right to family life. He says he has no family in Kosovo. Also he is mentally ill and will not get the treatment for his condition in Kosovo he gets here.

He is asked whether he has any family in Kosovo. He says he has two younger married sisters in the country, but when asked where his father is he says he is dead, adding. 'My father was killed by the man who appears in my mirror all the time.'

A report from a specialist is placed on file but the contents are not read out. Some pills are put on the desk in evidence. An argument then ensues about the quality of the mental health services in Kosovo. There appear to be no independent means of checking the statements made on either side, that there is a primary care service in Kosovo, or that Albanians are not offered hospital treatment for mental disorders.

A Judgement of Solomon

It is impossible to tell the truth of any of the stories you hear, although the bench makes heroic efforts to do so. What the courts are looking at are random slices of life in the Third World. Courts often rely on reports by various non-governmental agencies on conditions in a particular country, on press reports or on UN papers. They are not universally reliable or up-to-date.

However despite the unpreparedness of many Home Office lawyers or presenting officers, it makes good sense for the appellant to be well prepared. Usually the taxpayer pays for your lawyer. But if he is not very good, it is worth going private. A good lawyer costs no more than an accountant. He is gaining for you a lifetime of guaranteed social security, the right to work, and a new passport. Moreover, the chances of success are high. The Home Office had until very recently begun to scale down the number of lawyers and barristers it would pay to oppose even the most fraudulent cases. Moreover, barristers' chambers are reluctant, even for a private fee of £650, to send lawyers to plead for the Home Office. Trying to stop migrants coming into Britain is not popular. Acting for an asylum seeker is, on the other hand, popular and lucrative.

One is also struck by the fact that, even in cases in which one suspects the applicant is lying or likely to abscond, no bail is posted, no court tipstaff takes the appellant away. People just drift through the doors back into ordinary life. It is too easy to vanish. Getting into Britain through a door held wide open by lawyers, political correctness and vociferous race relations lobbies is as easy as brushing aside a tattered curtain.

Quis Custodiet?

Although all lawyers and advisers have now to be checked and registered, this was an area in which previously malpractice and fraud were commonplace. The Lord Chancellor's Office reported in 1998:

> ...bogus advisers charge for filling in forms, charge for arranging false marriages and providing details of false political asylum applications, charge for arranging temporary national insurance numbers, disposal of passports and other documentation... Charges may vary from tens of pounds for forms and form filling, through hundreds for nationality applications, to thousands for false asylum/marriage etc applications.[3]

Things have improved since the government introduced the Office of the Immigration Services Commissioner

(OISC). It is no longer possible to represent a client or advise him unless you are registered with the OISC.

But it would be naive to assume that everybody now goes to a registered adviser first, and there is no way of knowing how many unregistered middlemen stand in the way of a migrant before he finds a lawyer or a registered adviser. Migrants are often frightened, unable to speak the language, and in no position to argue.

But it is not all gloom. The author, posing as somebody who needed immigration advice, rang an adviser who had been exposed in the press for coaching witnesses and offering to buy passports. The switchboard operator burst into giggles. 'He is in prison', she announced.

7

Counting them in

To anyone over the age of 55 walking down a London street, it is obvious that in the last 30 years a huge settlement of foreigners has occurred. The word 'foreigner' however is a misconception. Many are the children or grandchildren of original immigrants who were born here. They are as British as the 55-year-old.

Such toleration has not been applied to another great settlement, that of Europeans in Africa and Asia during the colonial period. Europeans, we are told, had no right to settle in Africa or India because they were there without the permission of the aboriginal populations. But has the settlement of Britain been with the consent of our aboriginal population? The British after all have never said: 'We would like large numbers of immigrants to come and settle in Britain'.

In some cases the process has been concealed. The *Observer* reported in 1998, one year after a Labour administration came into power, that:

> Britain has quietly lifted the barriers to refugees from oppressive regimes, allowing them to stay despite the Government's tough anti-immigration rhetoric. Human rights groups have welcomed the rise in successful refugee application—one in five was approved during the first eight months of this year, compared with one in ten over the past ten years. But they and the Home Office have kept quiet about the rise for fear of a backlash against asylum seekers...

Jan Shaw, Refugees Officer for Amnesty International, said:

> There has been an enormous rise in those granted refugee status. We are not making much of it because we want the government to continue paying regard to human rights.[1]

The public, it seems, are not competent to decide who should come and live in Britain. This type of political conviction, coupled with poor immigration control, a lack of definition of who has a right to settle in Britain, political expediency and outright denial, have all played their part.

The result has been the arrival, since 1960, of several large and fairly distinct ethnic groups numbering some 4.5 million people. If present rates of migration continue, by 2050 whites will be the minority in the capital. By 2100 they will be a minority in the entire country.[2]

We are already rewriting our history to take account of the new settlers. While multi-culturalism and ethnic authenticity are welcomed, the word British is either frowned on or demands are made for its meaning to be altered. Britain and even 'Britishness' we are told is an artefact.

In October 2000 the Commission on the Future of Multi-Ethnic Britain published its report, known as the Parekh Report, which asked for Britain to be declared a multi-cultural and multi-faith society, by which it appears they meant a multi-racial society with no special acknowledgement being made to the British. Britain should recast its national history as a nation of ex-slavers and exploiters ruling a variety of helots.

Some of the evidence supplied to Lord Parekh and his commissioners came from a survey conducted by the Commission on Racial Equality, asking people what it meant to be British. Some of the replies, used as epigraphs to the chapters of the Parekh Report, were striking:

> The future of Britain lies in the hands of … descendants of slave owners and slaves, of indentured labourers, of feudal landlords and serfs, of industrialists and factory workers, of lairds and crofters, of refugees and asylum-seekers.[3]

Britain should forget important parts of its history:

> The Rule Britannia mindset, given full-blown expression at the Last Night of the Proms and until recently at the start of programming each day on BBC Radio 4, is a major part of the problem of Britain. In the same way that it continues to fight the Second World War … Britain seems incapable of shaking off its imperialist identity. The Brits do appear to believe that 'Britons never, never, never shall be slaves' … [But] it is impossible to colonise three-

fifths of the world ... without enslaving oneself. Our problem has been that Britain has never understood itself and has steadfastly refused to see and understand itself through the prism of our experience of it, here and in its coloniser mode.[4]

Numbers

MigrationwatchUK—a UK think tank—predicts that if current trends continue, Britain can expect a net inflow of two million people from outside the EU per decade.[5]

Since the year 2000 there has been a sharp rise in the number of people seeking asylum in the UK. In the mid-1990s we were receiving around 30,000 applications a year. This number jumped to 80,000 in 2000,[6] and has, with small ups and downs, remained around that level since.

We are now the favourite choice of asylum seekers heading for Europe. 'Britain topped the list in 2000 with 81,000 applications (UNHCR figures). Germany had 65,000, Belgium 38,000, France 37,000 and Netherlands 36,000. Until 1988, by contrast, numbers applying in the UK seldom exceeded 5,000 per year. Most applicants at that time went to Germany.'[7]

More family members can come later. In the past ten years, ten per cent of applicants were granted asylum, 17 per cent were given exceptional leave to remain and 12 per cent were removed. Some 50,000 to 60,000 a year disappear.

One independent means of checking the numbers coming to Britain is the International Passenger Survey. Questioners sample 0.2 per cent of passengers entering and leaving Britain each year. They ask when they arrived, for what purpose, from where and how long they intend to stay.

In the year 2000 the IPS estimated that Britain had gained 183,000 new settlers, about the same as the previous three years, but double that between 1990 and 1994.

Two groups are not included: those who enter the UK legally on student visas or as tourists and vanish, and those who enter Britain secretly and never declare themselves. The most conservative estimate suggests that 35,000 enter the country as tourists or students, and some 25,000 arrive as clandestines.

Some suspect this figure is far higher. Until very recently, when, following intense media scrutiny, security was stepped up at Calais, there was evidence that large numbers of people were secretly slipping into the UK completely unknown to the authorities to join a well organised black-market economy.

Harriet Sergeant, in her book *Welcome to the Asylum*, recalls that during the three days prior to a visit she made to Dover in 1998, customs officers at the port discovered 273 migrants hidden in trucks. Yet only 10 per cent of trucks were searched.[8] At Dover ferries arrive 24 hours a day at forty-five minute intervals. Each ferry can carry between 60 and 70 trucks.

However, such a 'catch' of refugees over three days is too small a period from which to draw a yearly average. To do that would require a properly conducted sampling exercise. This has never been done. There are huge difficulties, one of which is that the searches are not random. As Sergeant relates:

> When immigrants are discovered, immigration officers have to stop searching in order to fill in 'a mountain of paperwork'. The Romanian and Afghan gangs who have cornered this particular market are well aware of this and immigration officers often receive anonymous tip offs. While the search team is tied up for several hours, the gangs are taking the opportunity to smuggle more customers on to the next ferry.[9]

People smugglers are certainly capable of such well-organised 'sting' operations.

> The gangs have infrastructures, communications and surveillance capabilities far in excess of anything that the law enforcement agencies in transit and source countries can muster, and the ease with which they operate across international boundaries means that the chances of their activities diminishing is negligible.[10]

What is not clear about these huge numbers—if they are true—is why the new arrivals would not immediately declare themselves to the authorities. If they do so they are guaranteed welfare and housing benefit. It may be that they are told by the gangs that if they surrender themselves to the authorities they will be deported, or they are threatened with violence if they try to declare themselves. For some it might be easier to enter the black economy than to try and gain asylum, for others it might be easier to enter the legal economy with false papers sold as a package by the gangs. At least until last year, you could always leave.

Alem, 29, an Albanian waiter in north London, came to Britain on a freight train in 1999 after paying smugglers £1,995. In the past year, while appealing the Home Office's rejection of his asylum application, he has traveled in and out of Britain illegally four times. 'In June last year my mother told me that my younger brother was getting married and I decided to surprise him', said Alem. 'It was easy getting out of Britain. We partied for three days, but then I had to get back because I had to return to work. We got into an equipment box on a train to England and, after that, we were okay. The train again stopped near Calais but nobody touched us. We even came out to stretch our legs. When we got to England, we jumped out and found a train station where we could get to London. I was one day late for work but my boss let me stay in the job.' He also travelled to Albania, hiding in a lorry, for his father's funeral, before returning to Britain by freight train.[11]

One very useful way of checking how many stay and how many people are leaving the UK would be to issue embarkation cards. These are a useful check on social security fraud, multiple asylum claims for benefit, false tourists and bogus students. With a reasonable computer system and embarkation cards it would be possible to track down overstayers. We used to have such a system, but the Labour government stopped issuing cards in 1999.

A Romanian maths teacher worked here for four years. She had entered on a tourist visa, overstayed her time and had taken a job as a cleaner in a hotel. The hotel, owned by an Indian, paid her £3 an hour. No tax or social security was deducted from her pay. She realised that once she returned home the Romanian authorities would confiscate her passport for five years for overstaying her tourist permit. She approached a refugee organisation with her problem, but although she was well qualified to teach in the UK and there is a huge shortage of mathematics teachers, she was told an exception would not be made. Friends made enquiries at the Home Office and received the same answer. She slipped out of Britain this year.[12]

Her stay here, with all the useful information it contains, including tax and social security fraud and the fact we are losing valuable talents, has gone unrecorded.

Why the Confusion?

There is a reluctance by the government to advertise the true extent of asylum seeking or the difficulties of controlling it.

> The Government Actuary Department has estimated that the net inflow of migrants will fall to 135,000 by the middle of the decade, but there is considerable doubt about this. Two years ago the department was working on estimates of a net inflow of 95,000 a year.[13]

This is because illegal settlement, like a successful burglary where the victim fails to notice that he has been burgled, is hard to detect. The items stolen by the man who is here illegally—health, education and social security benefits—go unmissed among the millions of genuine claims made each year. Like domestic thefts in a rented block of flats, the landlord of the burgled house, in this case the Government, would rather keep quiet about them. There is little point in advertising that the country's doors are wide open.

Matters are not helped by the government's insistence that those who have been accepted for settlement, or issued with passports, are no longer classed as asylum seekers. Naturalisation, it is said, is one of the easiest ways of reducing illegal migration. Reclassifying asylum seekers also conceals the long-term consequences. Thus relatives coming to join those who were once asylum seekers but have now been accepted for settlement or citizenship are not classed as asylum seekers, but nevertheless are a direct consequence of asylum seeking. Perhaps a new term 'settler' should be introduced, covering the whole process of asylum, including the arrival of family members.

Compounding this is the fact that the Home Office immigration service has been one of the worst-run divisions of the British Civil Service (although there are now some signs of improvement). Massive computer failures, incompetence, lost files, and unwieldy and often impenetrable statistics (the statistics have improved slightly of late) leave few observers with any confidence in the service.

'They [the British Civil Service] don't like trouble,' said an immigration officer. 'And they do not like dealing with people. This is in contrast to France where the courts will back the state against the citizen, and back it even more so against a foreigner.'[14]

How Much Does It Cost?

The bill for the first day of an asylum seeker's arrival comes to £600.[15] He has to be interviewed by immigration officers with an interpreter present, and each question and answer written down in long hand and read back to the interviewee to make sure he understands it. He has to be photographed, fingerprinted and given a health check.

The asylum seeker then enters a world of lawyers, private landlords, work-brokers, charities and benefit agencies. The first people he will meet after his interview with immigration officers are charity case-workers. Many of these organisations receive government grants. In 1998 the Refugee Legal Aid Centre and the Immigration Advisory Service together received £6.7 million in grants.[16] The case-workers will arrange emergency accommodation for the asylum seeker, provide him with pocket money and a ticket to London. They will also advise him on how to obtain legal aid.

Legal aid for immigration cases came to £138 million in 2001-02, making it by far the largest category (see figure 6 p. 54). It had increased by 237 per cent in one year, and is estimated to be about to increase by another 15 per cent to £160 million in 2002-03.[17]

Lawyers charge around £500 for the first interview and basic paperwork. Touts haunt the arrival areas at our airports and docks. Some seem to have foreknowledge of a migrant's arrival, even if it is in the back of a truck. Later, at appeals, charges can rise to up to £650 for a court appearance by a barrister.

In addition to legal costs, welfare benefits for an average migrant family costs £8,150 a year. Housing costs can be as high as £500 per family per week, which can be reclaimed as benefit. A council tax benefit of £468 is paid per year to each single adult. The education of one child costs a further £1,600. NHS costs for GP care are £200 a year per refugee, 30 per cent more than an indigenous Briton.[18]

Figure 6
Expenditure on Legal Help Analysed by Category of Law

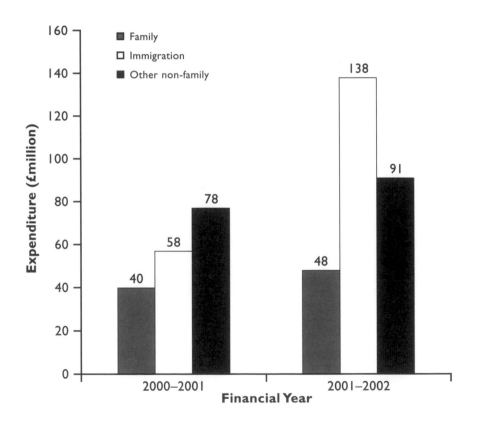

Source: National Audit Office analysis of Legal Services Commission data in *Community Legal Service: The introduction of contracting*, London: National Audit Office, November 2002, p. 8.

A further £40 million is spent in pursuing migrants who abscond.[19] Those who are found are then offered tickets home at an average of £680 per head. Those who refuse to leave voluntarily can be physically deported. This can involve expensive detention facilities, last minute legal appeals, the use of escorting officers, complicated negotiations with the destination country, some countries have been known to refuse at the last minute to take deportees, and the cost of aircraft seats or aircraft and other transportation. Further unquantifiable costs include tax evasion, housing and benefit fraud and multiple 'phantom' applications for asylum.

The Immigration Service Union concluded that the cost of asylum seeking in 1998 was £2.1 billion pounds, or 1p on the rate of income tax. This did not include those who entered and were never detected by the authorities. Since this figure was calculated the number of asylum seekers has nearly doubled.

8

Deportation: bailing with a colander

'Get them out!' screamed a headline in the *Daily Express*.[1] Below was a story of 20,000 asylum seekers who, having been refused permission to settle here, had not been deported.

But it is not that easy. Three problems get in the way of an effective deportation policy: finding the deportee, finding a country that will take him back, and finding the money to pay for his deportation.

There is much brave talk, and even braver Home Office statistics, about the numbers of people removed from Britain. A favourite word is 'removal', conjuring up a picture of court orders and immigration officers knocking on peoples' doors. Figure 7 (p. 57) gives one a comforting sense of things under control. But the term removal is mendacious.

Removal can mean lots of things. An American businessman arrives in Britain and finds that his visa will not cover the length of his stay. He needs two or three more days to complete some business. The immigration officer issues him with a notice to leave the country that just 'happens' to coincide with the new date of his return. This, related an immigration officer, can be classed as a 'removal'. It has nothing to do with asylum seeking or illegal migration.

Applied to 'real' illegal immigrants the term is even more confusing. The Home Office tells us that:

Some 69,875 illegal entrants who entered the country clandestinely or by deception were served with papers in 2001.[2]

But only 10,290 were removed:

Deportations fell by 65 per cent compared to 2000, and administrative removals rose substantially, largely due to the re-categorisation of certain types of immigration offenders from deportation to administrative removal.[3]

56

Figure 7
Asylum Seekers Removed

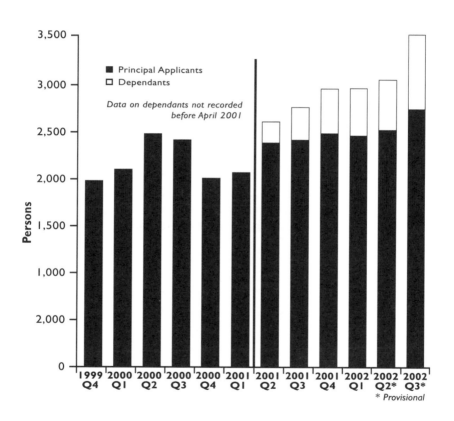

Source: *Home Office Asylum Statistics: 4th Quarter 2001, United Kingdom*, p. 6; *Home Office Asylum Statistics: 3rd Quarter 2002, United Kingdom*, p. 6.

Another comforting phrase found in official statistics is 'initiating an action against a refused person'. This conjures up pictures of immigration snatch squads hiding behind a hedge waiting to seize an overstayer. In reality, it means sending letters to those who should not be here telling them they should leave the country. Unsurprisingly, most overstayers move house and leave no forwarding address.

A few, however, are persuaded to leave by the offer to pay their air fares home. Of the 130,000 illegal overstayers known to the government in 2000, some 7,000 left with tickets paid for by the government. The cost per person was on average £680. Resettlement allowances of £2,700 per family are now (2002) being offered to families returning to Afghanistan.

'Real' deportations are few and far between. Immigration officers speak of a 'handful' every month, others of around 200 a year. There is a backlog of some 130,000 deportees waiting to be sent home. A jumbo jet would have to leave Heathrow each day for a year, filled with refugees, to clear it.

Finally there is the problem of where to send refugees. The Balkans present no difficulty. Recently defeated by European and US troops, they will take whoever we send. But many countries do not want their citizens back. Questions are raised about lack of documentation, and many refugees destroy their papers so they cannot be sent home. Some countries ask for money. The Irish government was forced to come to an agreement with the Nigerian government over the repatriation of migrants.[4] With 500 Nigerians awaiting deportation from Ireland in August 2001,[5] it was reported that the Irish Minister for Justice, John O'Donoghue, had signed a pact with the Nigerian government promising £7 million sterling for 'enhancement of aid' in return for speeding up the deportations.

Ireland, which has a repatriation deal with Romania, was at the time planning to make similar arrangements with Poland and Bulgaria.

The Irish government's move would seem, on the face of it, pragmatic and sensible. Only 15 per cent of all asylum seekers arriving in Ireland meet the criteria for being granted asylum, so Ireland gets rid of its unwelcome guests, and Nigeria gets more aid. But it is 'Danegeld'. Given Nigeria's record of corruption, it will not be long before more 'migrants' start arriving in the hope of getting further 'aid'.

The deal was condemned by Euro MP Patricia Mckenna who said: 'Basically they are bribing the Lagos Government to take these people back.' She criticised the Irish government because Nigeria was 'an unsafe country' where between 400 and 500 people had died in racial violence.[6] Whether that meant that all of Nigeria's 126,635,626 million population was entitled to asylum in Ireland was something Ms Mckenna did not specify.

'Reform'

At intervals home secretaries appear before the House of Commons promising to be tough on bogus asylum seekers. Such statements have a Gilbertean ring: 'I've got him on the list.' In 1999 Jack Straw promised that the 170 hijackers who seized an Afghan airliner in February 2000 would be sent home. The cost of looking after them, including trying those who seized the airliner, is said to stand at over £4 million. Half are still here.[7]

More general statements have met with as little success. On coming to power in 1997, the Labour government produced a policy called Firmer, Faster, Fairer. It promised asylum seekers would be given vouchers instead of cash, and, to prevent overcrowding and ethnic tension, they would be dispersed to cities and small towns all over Britain, rather than being allowed to wander at will.

It made no dent whatsoever in the number of people coming. Two years into office, the backlog of asylum seekers was growing by 3,000 a month, 450 immigration staff had resigned, and a new computerised system bought by the previous administration had collapsed.

Vouchers were worth £36.54 per week for a single person over 25, of which £10 was in cash. The scheme was administered by a private firm called Sodhexo to which the Home Office paid around £2.1 million pounds over two years.[8] Opposition to vouchers was immediate, instant and very loud, not because of Sodhexo's profits, but on principle.

There is no justifiable reason why a group of people lawfully present in the UK, and to whom the UK owes a number of legal and moral obligations, should be denied access to a level of support regarded as society's safety net... Oxfam is therefore deeply concerned that the 1999 Immigration and Asylum Act condemns these desperate people—many of whom have a genuine fear of persecution—to live in extreme poverty in Britain.[9]

In reality each asylum seeker was (and is) entitled to free accommodation in the UK paid for by local authorities, free education for their children, free health care, free legal aid, free travel to their new homes and, in the case of pregnant mothers, a maternity grant of £300.

One would have thought that, given such generosity, carping about vouchers was small-minded. British citizens on full income support only receive £19 a week more than an asylum seeker. Moreover, most asylum seekers (80 per cent) are fit young men sent by families who can afford £6,000 to pay a gang. Only nine per cent are the piteous victims of persecution that Oxfam and other agencies portray.

But making this distinction is to misunderstand the politics of asylum seeking in Britain. Refugee agencies make no distinction between an asylum seeker and a British citizen. Both are entitled to the same rights. Press pressure continued against the voucher system, and in October 2001 it was scrapped. The numbers of asylum seekers since that date have sharply increased.

Dispersal also met with difficulties after the stabbing of a refugee in a Glasgow slum, and after the resolute refusal of Gloucestershire and Somerset villagers to accept asylum hostels, attempts to disperse migrants were, for a while, quietly dropped. 'Firmer, Faster, Fairer' died. Renewed attempts to disperse refugees are meeting with similar resistance from rural populations.

September 11

If the government had hoped that asylum had been quietly buried, September 11 revived it. People in the US were angered to learn that student visa approval forms were sent to two of the dead hijackers, Mohammed Atta and Marwan Al-Shehhi, exactly six months after the attacks on the twin towers. Both Atta, of Egypt, and Al-Shehhi, of the United Arab Emirates, originally entered the United States on visitors' visas.[10] Suddenly the world could see how easy it was for terrorists to fly in and out of any country they chose.

A new British policy announced by Home Secretary David Blunkett, Secure Borders, Safe Haven, outlined fresh attempts to speed up asylum applications, promised new methods of detecting fraudulent applications, and outlined plans to make social security conditional on attending clearance centres. Immigration officers would be able to refuse entry to people who were listed as suspected terrorists. Secure units would be built for those the government intended to deport or who were likely to abscond before their claims were properly examined. Language tests, and an oath of loyalty, were be instituted. Migrants would have to sign up to the idea of being British.

But at the same time the Home Secretary, still wedded to the idea of a shortage of workers, announced that we would be allowing in large numbers of unskilled workers under work permits. More young people on temporary visas from Commonwealth countries were to be allowed in, but the emphasis would be on the new Commonwealth (black) countries as against old Commonwealth (white) countries. The programme of allowing highly qualified workers into the country would be continued and expanded.

Since the proposals, the numbers of asylum seekers trying to storm Channel Tunnel freight trains has increased, causing it to be temporarily shut at a loss of £555,000 a week. Yarlswood Detention Centre in Bedfordshire, a key documentation holding unit, was destroyed by fire in mysterious circumstances in February 2002. Vital records were destroyed and insurers are proving reluctant to cover other such facilities although now they are taking detainees.[11] In March David Blunkett ran into a storm of criticism for his use of the word 'swamped' when describing the difficulties schools have in areas where there are large numbers of asylum seekers. Attitudes have changed little.

Now his latest proposals to send back asylum seekers with manifestly unfounded claims will face the same test. For a while they may work, but the Human Rights Act (see below the case of the Afghan refugees deported to Germany) and the sheer drip of political correctness on the public mind, will erode the confidence and determination of the Home Office. If some tremendous disaster occurs, like a nuclear war in India, most of these rules will be laid aside and not picked up again.

In any event, the changes to the rules on migrant workers, the steady flow of spouses of migrants already here, the admission of 'key' workers and the pernicious idea that our economy will collapse unless we admit large numbers of unskilled workers, will make up for any restriction of present flows. The question we have to consider is not how immigrants get here, but whether we should take them at all.

9

Why immigration should be controlled

People trafficking is a type of modern slavery. Often run by violent gangs it is linked to criminal activities such as drug smuggling, prostitution and extortion.

We grant a few applicants delivered by traffickers full asylum, some we allow to remain because they come from such awful countries we would not sleep well at night if we sent them back, the rest we tell to leave. But we make no serious effort to expel those in the last category. Often illegally employed, they are forced to live under false identities without proper access to the law or the freedoms which we enjoy.

They join a large but unknown number of illegal immigrants, smuggled into Britain, who never come to the attention of the authorities. We delude ourselves that we need all these people because we do not have sufficient of our own to fill gaps in the labour market. We would of course like to improve their conditions, but they are victims of an economic imperative, derived from an ageing population and labour market shortages.

Many become second-level slaves, ruthlessly exploited by other migrants. The high prices Westerners pay for food and services are often not passed on to terrified clandestines sweating in kitchens or working long hours in sewing factories. Middlemen, often migrants themselves, take everything.

The National Criminal Intelligence Service reports that:

Often the amount [the price for being smuggled in Britain] agreed in the source country is increased once the entrants reach the UK. Because they are here illegally, they do not approach the authorities and are ripe for extortion and exploitation. There are plenty of examples of entrants who don't pay up being faced with extreme violence.

Repayment for the journey or other services once in the country (such as accommodation) can involve very menial and low paid labour, and long hours, such as in sweat shops, cleaning or in restaurants. Women are also trafficked for involvement in prostitution.

Sometimes organised criminals bring over females specifically to work as prostitutes, keeping them virtually as prisoners here in the UK.[1]

One type of trafficking supports the other. Some migrants pay gangs to get them into Britain and then apply for asylum. This bankrolls further smuggling, often of people so terrified of being deported, and ignorant of British law, that they remain in hiding and under control of the gangs, exploited for their labour or worse.

Unless we take extremely robust action to deport illegal arrivals as soon as they set foot in Britain, which, as we will see later, requires us to reform or scrap the Human Rights Act, we will never stamp this activity out. The source of illegal migrants is almost limitless. Even a policy of bringing people in on work permits will not stop an expansion of the smuggling trade. People-smuggling is about delivering cheap labour to a market. Smugglers will always be able to do it cheaper than governments, and if they can't they will just dump the surplus on our doorstep, or lure their victims into crime.

Moreover the reason we tolerate it—that we are trying to fill an alleged gap in our labour markets because of our ageing population—is based on a demographic fallacy.

Filling the Age Gap

A UN report on replacement migration suggests how many migrants the West would require to maintain the present ratio of workers to pensioners.[2] It is a simple and attractive idea but, as with many simple ideas, probably wrong.

Central to its argument is the notion that the problem of ageing in Western populations can be solved by bringing in younger migrants. This would take Britain back to a golden age when young people thronged the streets and there were plenty of willing hands to look after the elderly, drive our buses, fill our factories and provide us with enough soldiers and police.

Figure 8
Average Household Size by Ethnicity,
1991-1996, Great Britain

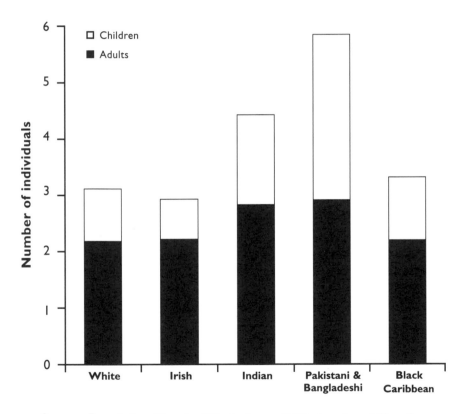

Source: *Population Trends 101,* Autumn 2000, London: Office for National Statistics, p. 13.

But for this to work its magic and maintain our support ratios, huge and rising numbers of immigrants have to be imported. The most extreme example of this would be Korea. David Coleman observes: 'Preserving the present support ratio of Korea would require the entire world population to go to live there by 2050.[3] Even the gangs might not be able to fill such an order.

This is because migrants, like everybody else, age. Importing them into a world where contraception is easily available and free, soon brings their birthrate close to ours. Contraception is catching. Populations of dependent elderly people looked after by fewer younger people are the future for the human race, unless we ban contraceptives, outlaw antibiotics, abandon vaccines, give up industrial agriculture and stop chlorinating water.

Figure 8 (p. 65) shows that the longer migrants have been here, the fewer children they have.[4] Whites and Irish have small families, West Indian families are getting like them, and Indians, as they assimilate, are following suit. The exceptions are Pakistani and Bangladeshi migrants, who arrived more recently.

The reasons are many. It could be construed that high birthrates mean poor assimilation and that is all that needs to be said. But it is useful to examine some of the possible reasons why one community has higher birthrates than another.

A very strong factor may be the presence of elderly relatives, grandparents and uncles, enforcing traditional values. A Bangladeshi marriage is much more internalised than a Western marriage, representing as it does the union of two families rather than two individuals.[5] In addition, the language barrier among older, poor Bangladeshis and Pakistanis, fuelled by a fear of the West and its alien values, can be formidable. Furthermore, migrants from countries like Bangladesh, with high infant mortality rates, have a tradition of large family size.

It is almost unknown for migrant groups not to begin marrying out sooner or later. Migrants assimilate, and with assimilation comes a fall in the birthrate. Contraception creates ageing populations. This runs counter to the widespread belief that migrants will arrest the ageing of aboriginal European populations.

As these new populations age, they will, like the ageing members of the European population alongside them, start to draw heavily on social security and funds for medical care. Some will have spent a full working life here, and will be 'paid up'. Those who have only lived here a short time, or are elderly or infirm, will not have contributed as much to the insurance funds. Those who have not been in the tax system because of lax immigration controls or lack of internal controls will be an uninsured charge on the state. It is an illusion, therefore, to think of immigrants as perpetually young, doing jobs that decrepit Europeans can no longer undertake. David Coleman writes:

> No well-informed organisation or government should entertain this notion, [that migration will solve the problem of supporting our elderly] which many demographic simulations have already shown to be impossible to achieve except at the cost of unsustainably high population rates.[6]

Nor are 'replacement' migrants cheap. In June 2002 it was announced by the Immigration and Nationality Directorate that the costs of supporting asylum seekers had risen in 2001 from an estimated £403 million to £1,052 million. The shortfall was on course to reach £1 billion in 2002. These figures did not include costs for the NHS or legal aid. Oliver Letwin, Shadow Home Secretary, commented that the projected £1 billion overspend would pay for an extra 30,000 policemen.[7]

It seems extraordinary that we should be exposing ourselves to such costs when in Britain many people retire at 55, expecting the state to look after them for 25 years. Coleman writes: 'As the age of retirement in Europe is just under 60, there is plenty of scope for longer-term increases in working life as active life expectation increases.'[8] We could also make use of the two-and-a-half million people who would work if they could find work. Coleman also reminds us that:

> Only 62 per cent of the nominal 'active' population aged 15—64 is economically active ... it would only take an 0.8 per cent increase in the rate of growth of productivity to make up for the shortfall in labour caused by our low birthrate and lower dependency ratios.[9]

If we raised the retirement age to 70 and made more of our population work, we could have our doctors, nurses and police, and run our schools without inviting people into the country who, far from working, need to be supported from the public purse. It is not migration we need but curbs on social security, a less generous retirement policy, better tax policies and longer hours.

It is not only our country that suffers. Migration plunders the countries we take migrants from—doctors, nurses, engineers, computer experts, teachers and farmers—driving those left behind deeper into poverty. And those we do not want—the unskilled—can only expect a brief period of employment until the next economic downturn. Britain is not, like America in the 1880s, an open society with vast spaces waiting to absorb new migrants.

The greater danger is that we may be creating the same conditions that followed the emancipation of America's slaves. Once freed they were forgotten. Detached from economic life, they endured a century of want as share croppers or casual labourers. We, too, may be faced with people for whom we have no use, and whom we will try to forget. Coleman notes:

> It has yet to be shown that extraordinary general labour needs, over and above particular shortages noted above, are required in most European countries at least for the next two decades.[10]

The shortages Coleman remarked on were, among others, in IT. When the dot.com market collapsed in 2000, the market for IT workers collapsed with it. The British government is no longer issuing work permits for IT workers, a situation which would have seemed inconceivable two years ago.

Unskilled workers are at even greater risk. Capitalism proceeds by boom and bust. During recessions, the poor with few savings suffer badly. One solution is to try and increase social security payments by importing more and more family members. This creates small ghettoes in Britain of disaffected poor, cut off from the mainstream of political life. Nor do we yet know how deflation—bringing price cutting, wage reductions and unemployment—now starting in the West, will affect unskilled migrants. It badly affected Japan, where savings were high. Britain's savings are at an historical low.

Such considerations seem far from the economic calculations of the apostles of globalism. In 'It's Good for Them and Better for the Rest of Us', Michael Gove, writing in *The Times*, quotes the Harvard economist George Borjas: 'While it is true that immigration lowers the wages of the least skilled...it is also the case that the drain on the exchequer from migrant labour is often less than that of indigenous workers. They come to this country with their early years health and education costs already covered by the country of origin.'[11]

This does not take into account the finding that in Europe, 'existing foreign populations... already feature prominently in unemployment figures, suffering, with important exceptions such as Italy, between 50 per cent and 300 per cent higher unemployment than the local population.'[12]

Moreover the theory that mass migration is of universal benefit flies in the face of history. The only comparable mass emigration to Britain in recent history, from Ireland in the nineteenth and twentieth centuries, deprived the country of its young people and left it economically disadvantaged. It was only when Ireland's young stopped leaving or began to return in the 1970s and the 1980s that Ireland began its remarkable recovery.

Nor is it just a matter of money. Somehow we have, like our eighteenth century forebears, become blind to the misery of migration, to the pain of loss of country and friends and the destruction of cultures. Migration is not the same as going on a package holiday. It can wreck lives, both here and in the countries migrants come from.

Imagine you live in a Third World country. Your child is very ill and you have to take him every month to a clinic twenty miles away for treatment. To get there you have to take a bus, and when you arrive the child has to have X-rays and blood tests, a fresh supply of drugs and an examination by a doctor. You are very poor but, thank God, you have saved enough to pay for the treatment.

Then you arrive one day to find the clinic boarded up. A notice over the door says that, due to staff shortages, the nearest clinic is now in the city, two days' bus journey away. The cost of a bus ticket is the same as a month's treatment. Later you hear that the clinic has shut because two of the nurses have gone to England. There they look after old people in a special hospital, people so old you would never see such a person in your country. Your child is five when he dies.

10

Law reform

The Immigration Appeals Tribunal oversees decisions made on asylum cases. Cases are frequently sent to it. The decisions its senior judges make open and close the doors of our frontiers to whole classes of asylum seekers. They are, however, virtual doors, because no means has yet been devised of physically enforcing asylum law to any meaningful extent. Politicians will not grasp the nettle of deportation.

In the face of political inaction, judges and lawyers have the last word on who can come and who must go. Interpretations of the Human Rights Act in the courts, written in dense legalese, with many a courteous reference to the decisions of other learned friends, and to the quiet fall of refreshers, carry far more weight than any speech David Blunkett might give.

Lately the appeals tribunals appear to be trying to bring common sense to decisions on asylum, and judges have reminded adjudicators that documents produced by refugees might not be genuine:

> [I]t is necessary to shake off any preconception that official looking documents are genuine, based on experience of documents in the United Kingdom, and approach them with an open mind. In asylum and human rights cases it is for an individual claimant to show that a document on which he seeks to rely can be relied on...[1]

It seems astonishing that this needs to be said.

In another case the judges ruled that it was up to asylum seekers to produce evidence supporting their case to be allowed to stay in Britain. If, for example, they did not put in an appearance at court—as in the case under appeal —the case could be decided against them.[2] One wonders on what basis appeals were heard before.

In another, the Appeals Tribunal ruled that, because a country had a history of abusing human rights, that did not mean the individual did not have to prove that he or she was at real risk.[3] Mere speculation was not enough. But as one set of judges labours to close the asylum door, another judge pushes it open.

In June 2001 a family of Afghan asylum seekers entered Britain using false names, complaining that they had been badly treated in Germany, the country where they had first sought refuge. Their claim was deemed to be 'manifestly unfounded' by the Home Secretary and with great publicity —they had sought refuge in a mosque from which they were forcibly removed by the police—they were deported back to Germany. The deportation cost £30,000. Newspapers reported that the Germans had rejected the family's claim to asylum and this was the reason why they had come to Britain.[4] Moreover, the case had been reviewed by no less than six separate judges, all of whom thought the Home Office was right to order them to leave.[5]

However, at judicial review, Mr Justice Scott Baker ruled they had a right to remain in Britain while their claim was heard by an independent adjudicator. He disputed Mr Blunkett's claim that the family had rights of residence and full access to social security and welfare provisions in Germany. The husband, Mr Ahmadi, was not allowed to work, they had 'tolerated' status not residence, and had to live in an asylum centre on minimal social security benefits. He was worried about the mental health of the mother and child. He ordered the case to be heard in front of an independent adjudicator with the evidence of the family being transmitted by video to London. Medical experts will be flown out to Germany to assess their condition at the taxpayers' expense.

It will be a landmark decision. Section 8 of the Human Rights Act, under which the family's claim is being made, guarantees the right to privacy and family life. If you cannot enjoy privacy and family life in one country, you can presumably go to another where you can.

Appeals under Section 8 of the Act are invoked by asylum seekers who have been here for a while, whose children are at school here, who have formed a network of friends and relatives, or are undergoing medical treatment. It is an effective weapon against removal, especially for those who vanish from official view long enough to set up a family in Britain. It is a brave bench which orders children to be plucked from their schools, fathers from their work, and mothers from their kitchens to be returned to places like Croatia or Afghanistan.

Just as in criminal cases, procedural tricks are employed by lawyers to delay immigration investigations. Doctors complain that patients under investigation by the immigration authorities turn up asking for medical certificates which they have been coached by their lawyers to demand. This puts them in an impossible situation from which many lawyers know they cannot escape.

It is the idea that migration law is a type of game among lawyers, either conducted for money or political ends, that is so worrying. Just as justice seems to be a joke among some defence lawyers in juvenile proceedings, so in immigration law the idea of fairness, both to the migrant and to the country being asked to accept him, has no standing. Here is a country stupid enough to pass a set of laws that depend on notions of fairness, citizenship and duty. Let us proceed to exploit them. It is an attitude familiar to those who have watched court cases in Third World dictatorships, where the law is a joke, a means of making huge sums of money or the way to the presidential palace.

Frontiers

At present we have a twenty-first century transport system with nineteenth-century frontiers. Although physical frontiers vanished some years ago, we still mark yellow lines on airport floors and have people at desks examining passports. This has all the utility of a Beefeater guarding the Tower of London. It looks nice and gives tourists a thrill. We need physical symbols of our law standing at our frontier, but illegal immigration starts a long way from Heathrow. Modern frontiers start at the point of an immigrant's departure and continue to the doors of the work-place. With investigation units in the countries of departure we would have some check on who was leaving and how true their stories were.

But no asylum policy will work unless we are prepared to create a modern internal passport system based on finger-prints, DNA and iris scans linked to social security records and Inland Revenue records. It is sad that we should have to consider surrendering some of our most ancient liberties, but we did it in the Second World War when we were threatened with invasion.

The government is introducing legislation in its new immigration and asylum bill to make it compulsory for firms to check that their workers are not illegal migrants. One part of this is the introduction of smart applicant registration cards, or ARC-cards, which have 'Employment prohibited' stamped on them. Such a card is only as good as the legislation and the political will behind it. The Refugee Council has already voiced concerns. It fears it might become an entitlement card depriving unregistered mi-grants of health care and benefits. They have little to fear. Human rights legislation would soon sweep such a device away if it interfered with asylum seekers' rights, an area in which the government is no longer sovereign.

Nor is the history of policing sweat shops good. Until now, when health and safety inspectors or immigration officers have discovered them and closed them down, no further action is taken against the employers. The government, admitting prosecutions to date had been 'virtually non existent', promised in January 2002 to remedy this state of affairs by mounting 'some high-profile prosecutions'. A move, the report said, 'designed to flush out up to 500,000 illegal foreign workers'.[6]

A year later, there have been no high-profile cases. As with deportation, the great fear is of an accusation of racism. Also illegal working is diffuse, protean and well hidden. Parts of our economy, a lot of catering for example, depend on it. Laws controlling it will be as hard to enforce as those on deportation.

Illegal workers remain attractive to the underground economy in Britain. Paying no taxes and unhampered by any legal obligation to provide decent working conditions or hours, the presentation of a card stamped 'Employment prohibited' would be a reference. The paper variety of this card, the standard acknowledgment letter, did not stop illegal working.

Fighting Asylum Fraud

Listening to appeal tribunals in the lower courts, one is struck by the absurdity of many of the stories. 'I walked out of the prison, dressed as a nurse', announced one burly African. One was reminded of Mr Toad fleeing his dungeon. Who could possibly know if this story was true?

One can smile, but bogus asylum claims are a form of fraud. We should see them in the same light as income tax evasion or social security fraud. You cannot catch every fraudster, but you can make life singularly unpleasant for those you do catch.

No bogus asylum seeker should feel absolutely safe walking into court and telling any story that comes into his head or that his lawyers have rehearsed him in. Individual asylum appeals at present rest on shaky foundations. Courts tend to rely on the general evidence that a particular country has a bad human rights record. The only other thing they have to guide them is their impression of a witness's veracity. Objective evidence needed to prove an applicant's story conclusively may be 8,000 miles away. There should be an investigating officer stationed at embassies in countries whence many claims originate whose job would be to run an intelligence and evidence collecting unit checking asylum stories. Not every case would be examined in detail, but some taken at random would be investigated thoroughly. Many of the stories heard in courts would collapse on simple factual detail. The penalties for making fraudulent claims would be severe. Convicting 100 such people a year would prove cheaper than holding tens of thousands of suspect cases in asylum centres.

Students, tourists and other people who suddenly 'remember' a few weeks or months after they arrive that they are really refugees should not be allowed to apply for asylum. Entering Britain and subsequently declaring you are seeking asylum should be an offence punishable by a fine, imprisonment and deportation.

At present we cannot change our law because of the Human Rights Act. This is a law Britain should never have passed. We had no need. We already possessed our liberty under statute and common law. Passing the Human Rights Act was political posturing by the Labour Party. It has cost us a great deal of money, and has caused many refugees suffering. By repealing the Act with maximum publicity we will send a strong signal to the gangs that the feeding bowl has been taken away.

Repealing the Act or, more importantly, rewriting it so it only applies within the geographical boundaries of Europe, or within the United Kingdom, would give us the opportunity to develop our own laws on asylum.

Some are outlined below. We would aim to take about 5,000 genuine refugees a year. Parliament could renew a bill each year on the numbers.

Outside the Act we could make our own laws on who should get social security. We could also ban marriages designed to market the commodity of British nationality. We should create a white list of countries that are recognised as safe to return people to. India and Pakistan should be on it.

These measures would have a major effect. As one immigration inspector said: 'One migrant sent home is a small but powerful message to migrants not to come. Each retreat by the British government is a loud message to the smugglers to send more.'[7]

Reforms

The aim of an asylum system is to offer refuge to the persecuted. It should not be a means—even incidentally—of obtaining cheap labour from poor countries. An asylum seeker on arriving in this country should give a truthful account of his reasons for fleeing his homeland. If this is accepted he should be given public funds until he finds work. We should create a legal entity called a temporary citizen. This would apply to an individual who had satisfied the immigration authorities he was a genuine asylum seeker, or came from a country it was unsafe to go back to. Temporary citizens would be issued with passports renewable at yearly intervals. These would be different from the smart cards asylum seekers are now being issued with, which are a means of identification and a way of obtaining benefits. A temporary passport would have the same force as a full passport and would be an introduction to citizenship. On renewal each year the passport holder would have to show that the reasons he fled his country still existed. If they did not he would have to leave. A serious conviction would mean deportation. At the end of five years, if conditions were still bad the asylum seeker would be allowed to stay and be given UK citizenship. Marriage, family and children would not be a reason for allowing him to stay during the probationary period. Asylum is a grant of refuge, not citizenship.

Temporary citizenship would also apply to spouses, relatives and others coming to join a permanent citizen in Britain. A temporary passport would not be an entitlement card but a new definition of citizenship, a legal status that could be revoked at any time up to five years.

If an asylum seeker's story is felt to be untrue, he should be removed. If he contests the decision, he should be held in a detention centre, given a month to prepare an appeal, and, if his story is still not believed, he should be deported.

Although this seems fair, there are political and practical problems in carrying it out. These are:

1. *The Human Rights Act.* This is key to any reform of the asylum system. It should be repealed.

    The Act is the major cause of our asylum crisis, but its critics are at an immediate disadvantage. To be critical of human rights is to be critical of the right of free speech, the right to a fair trial, the right to freedom of assembly and religious belief, the right of people to marry whom they chose and the right to privacy and family life.

This is not the case. There is nothing wrong with the idea of universal human rights, but a lot wrong with the idea of enforcing them by law. For human rights are not universally applied. The West, because of its internal democratic principles, upholds human rights, not just for its own citizens but for everyone else. Anybody arriving in Britain who claims his or her rights have been violated elsewhere, and who can convince a court that they are telling the truth, has an absolute right to settle.

Yet those governments in the world who oppress their citizens are excused any such obligation. Indeed, it suits them that the West takes their more troublesome citizens. It allows them to go on stealing and looting from those who remain. Nor have such governments anything to fear from us. Our asylum courts cannot despatch investigators to arrest and bring back any of their police or officials who have persecuted an asylum seeker.

But you can no more have human rights for one part of the world and not the rest than you can have an income tax system in which people in small towns and villages are taxed while the inhabitants of cities are not.

The West today has no authority over upholding human rights in the Third World, but is being made to pay for the breach of them. We cannot oblige the governments of Iraq or Korea to uphold the human rights of their citizens, but we are obliged to take those who flee, if they turn up on our borders.

To apply universal human rights, we would need to return to a form of colonialism, something that very few human rights advocates would support. An independent international judiciary and police force would be required to arrest and prosecute violators. This would require the consent of the populations of places like Syria, Saudi Arabia or China. When international police arrived to arrest human rights violators, some of whom would almost certainly be leading members of their governments, they would have to be allowed to take them off to the International Court of Justice at the Hague without protest.

Legal demands based on the universality of human rights mean nothing if they cannot be universally enforced. Any law that cannot be universally applied will lead to poisonous resentment on the part of those who are forced to obey it.

We need to repeal the Human Rights Act, or re-write it so it can only be applied to those parts of the world where it can be enforced. This does not mean we have to stop taking asylum seekers, if they are genuine, but our obligation would be a moral one (and therefore stronger), not a legalistic one.

There are other lesser but still essential reforms which are required if we want to show we are serious about offering refuge to genuine asylum seekers.

2. *Our Lax Welfare System.* This is a major draw. Only those asylum seekers who declared themselves at the port would be allowed to draw social security. People who only 'remember' they want asylum after they have been in the country for a while would be barred from receiving funds.

3. *Deportation.* Many countries refuse to take asylum seekers back if they have no papers. Many asylum seekers know this and destroy their papers so they cannot be sent back. In addition there are countries, such as Iraq, which are unsafe to send anybody back to.

We need to deport a lot more people than we are presently doing, and not just to countries where we have troops such as the former Yugoslavia. Britain must maintain an extensive list of countries it is safe for asylum seekers to go back to. The farce of declaring France and Germany unsafe countries should be ended. The bilateral agreement with France should be restored. Making grants and preferential trade deals available to countries which are prepared to take their citizens back is good policy. Although opposed by other members of the EU, sanctioning countries which do not co-operate by withdrawing trade deals or setting up tariffs is vital.

4. *Other measures*. Creating the category of temporary citizen would make record-keeping easier. One of the reasons both politicians and the public have not been alerted to the problem is the unnecessary complexity of Home Office statistics. All manner of categories of settler have been created. There are asylum seekers, dependants who arrive with them, dependants who come after they have been granted leave to remain, spouses, relatives, people who have been given exceptional leave to remain, and so on. To add to the headache, the presentation of the figures can change from year to year.

5. *Prosecution*. Ten per cent of asylum cases should be investigated in depth. Those cases where outright fraud was discovered would go on to the criminal courts. Those where it was a question of opinion would go to the asylum appeal court.

6. *Work permits*. The present government sees work permits as an easy solution to an intractable problem. Issuing work permits, or 'managed migration' as it is called, will, ministers hope, cause asylum seeking to go away. It will not. Asylum seekers and work permit holders come from different places. Nor are work permits likely to be attractive to employers in areas like the catering industry which relies heavily on untaxed workers.

Far from decreasing the numbers of migrants, granting more work permits will only increase the number of migrants entering Britain, and it is not easy to see how this scheme can be properly policed. The projected numbers are large. 175,000 permits are provided for next year. Holders of these will able to bring in their families and ask for permanent residence after five years. We do not have the infrastructure to cope with such a massive influx.

Conclusion

To carry out any of these reforms would require a degree of political confidence that at present we do not possess. Once the most confident of peoples, we have been undermined by the fall of the empire and the 40 years of self-recrimination that followed. We have been told we are irredeemably racist and that our history is one of mass plunder of the globe. We are now so frightened of ourselves we fear to look in the mirror of history. Lately we have even been ashamed to speak our own name.

Confronting asylum seeking, with its undertones of racism and colonialism, makes us particularly anxious. So much so that we have allowed our politicians to sideline it until migrants began to actually storm our frontier with France. Even now we will not admit that we have almost no control over how many people are settling in Britain, and once they arrive we have no means of removing the very large number who should not be here and are abusing our hospitality. Instead we have decided that since they are here we probably need them, either to keep up our birthrate (impossible and unnecessary) or to replace our dwindling work force (also unnecessary).

We now have to make up our minds. Either we are a country with a limited capacity for taking in strangers, or we give up all pretence to nationhood and merge into a global frontierless world of shifting tribal loyalties.

That would be a tragedy. England is one of the great engines of democracy. Piece by piece we have assembled a society in which religious freedom, freedom of expression, the right to property and life have become so accepted that few give it a thought. Far from plundering the planet or being racist, we were foremost in exporting the industrial revolution to a fifth of the globe. Just under two hundred years ago we sent out British ships to destroy the world's slave trade.

It is a role that is not over. The future will depend on strong nation states which are determined to uphold representative democracy. We should take in some asylum seekers, perhaps ten per cent of all those who try to get in. Taking in large numbers of economic migrants because you cannot think of any good reason to keep them out, and not knowing who they are, or how many there are, is irresponsible and foolish. To try and avoid finding out who is living in your country is even madder. We need new types of passport, better frontier controls and citizenship rituals if we are to preserve our democracy. You cannot have a representative democracy unless you know who you are representing.

Above all we must repeal the Human Rights Act.

Politicians often talk of oaths of loyalty for refugees, but it is our own loyalty that we need to revive. We have something of great price to offer the world. To lose it, because we are so lacking in confidence that we no longer recognise it, would be an extraordinary tragedy, not just for us, but for those who really need our help, the world's dispossessed.

Nationalism and Liberalism: Friends or Foes?

David Conway

Acknowledgments

This paper has previously appeared in the *Journal of Libertarian Studies*, (vol. 16, no. 1, 2002, pp. 1-22). The author is grateful to the editor of that journal, Professor Hans Hermann-Hoppe for helpful comments on an earlier version of the paper. The paper was first delivered as the Mises Memorial Lecture at the Sixth Austrian Scholars' Conference organised under the auspices of the Ludwig von Mises Institute at Auburn, Alabama, in March 2000. The Ludwig von Mises Institute owns the copyright of the paper and it is reproduced here by kind permission.

Nationalism and Liberalism: Friends or Foes?

David Conway

1. Introduction

From time to time during the course of the twentieth century, eruptions of nationalist ardour and aspiration have resulted in great hardship and depredations being visited on various peoples of the world. Few peoples, if any, have escaped becoming engulfed in major conflicts arising from their own nationalistic aspirations or those of other peoples. In themselves, however, national pride and allegiance can seem not merely innocuous but positively benign. For, as well as sometimes as leading to war and conflict, such forms of attachment help also to foster a *prima facie* attractive cultural diversity among the different peoples of the world, as well as provide a sense of meaning, belonging, and pride which many people might otherwise have been without, as well as foster solidarity and civility among those who look on each other as being of the same nation. What should the attitude of classical liberals be towards nationalist aspiration and sentiment? Should they value and cultivate these attitudes in themselves and others—at least, in their ostensibly less xenophobic and aggressive forms? Or should they look on all forms and manifestations of nationalism as nothing more than an atavistic remnant of pre-modernity, outmoded forms of attachment which, ideally, should be expunged from humanity in favour of a cosmopolitan individualism the universal adoption of which will have marked the liberation of humanity from all divisive partial allegiances and attachments? Alternatively, should classical liberals regard nationalist sentiment and allegiance as being a purely private matter and as having nothing to do with their political outlook as such?

For a considerable time after the end of World War Two, classical liberal and libertarian writers paid comparatively little attention to the phenomenon of nationalism or, indeed, to international relations in general, save those issues directly connected with the Cold War and international trade. With the Cold War over, and with practically universal recognition having been gained, albeit often only grudgingly so, for the superior allocative efficiency of markets over central planning, a dramatic and somewhat unforeseen recent world-wide resurgence of various forms of nationalist aspiration and particularism has led both classical liberals and libertarians to turn their attention to the phenomenon of nationalism.

At first sight, the prospects for effecting a reconciliation between nationalism and classical liberalism seem bleak. With characteristic acumen, Friedrich Hayek has gone to the heart of the problem:

> The advocates of individual freedom have generally sympathised with ... aspirations for national freedom [that is: with the desire of peoples to be free from foreign yoke and to determine their own fate], and this has led to the constant but uneasy alliance between the liberal and the national movements during the nineteenth century. But though the conception of national freedom is analogous to that of individual freedom, it is not the same; and the striving for the first has not always enhanced the second. It has sometimes led people to prefer a despot of their own race to the liberal government of the alien majority; and it has often provided the pretext for ruthless restrictions of the individual liberty of minorities.[1]

Further, in his famous essay on why he is not to be thought of as a conservative, Hayek registers a second reservation about nationalism from a classical liberal perspective.

> Nationalistic bias frequently provides the bridge ... to collectivism: to think in terms of 'our' industry or resource is only a short step away from demanding that these national assets be directed in the national interest.[2]

In light of these concerns voiced by Hayek, we might feel there is little point in trying to effect any reconciliation between nationalism and classical liberalism.

Despite the undoubted truths contained in Hayek's msigivings, still it seems worthwhile to attempt such a reconciliation. For, however enlightened and cosmopolitan classical liberals may rightly consider themselves to be, and however illiberal and barbaric some manifestations of nationalism have undoubtedly been, there can be few classical liberals who, if honest with themselves, will not admit to harbouring deep within their breasts some form of nationalistic attachment and affiliation. These sentiments might only manifest themselves as some inarticulate love for the country and traditions of their birth and residence, combined with some weak and generalised affection for those whom they regard as their compatriots.

2. Terminological Prelude

I think we need hardly remind ourselves of an attachment to which ideals and values is to be thought of as constitutive of the classical liberal outlook. They include, most importantly, private property rights, minimal government, and, hence, maximum possible equal freedom of thought, expression, activity and association, together with constitutional representative government, division of powers, and the rule of law. It is not that much more difficult to form a relatively clear and distinct idea of what nationalism is. Against this term, the *Oxford English Dictionary* lists two distinct but related meanings. The first is *devotion to one's nation*; the second is *a policy of national independence*. Combining these two meanings, we arrive at the following definition of the term. 'Nationalism' denotes *the devotion felt by members of a nation towards their own nation, as well as the striving by members of a nation on behalf of its political independence, enjoyed, ideally, in that territory considered to be its traditional homeland.* We shall not be able to decide on the compatibility or otherwise with liberal ideals and values of this species of sentiment and aspiration without first obtaining a clear understanding of what a nation is.

What, then, are we to think of a nation as being? This question is by no means quite as straightforward as it appears at first glance. To see wherein the complexity lies, consider the following explication of the term once offered by Ayn Rand. She writes,

> A 'nation' is not a mystic or supernatural entity; it is a large number of individuals who live in the same geographical locality under the same political system.[3]

The first part of Rand's explication seems undoubtedly true; the second more questionable. Is it really true that all people residing in the same geographical locality under the same political system are members of the same nation as each other? Try telling that to the Serbs and ethnic Albanians in Kosova, or to the Palestinian Arabs and Jewish settlers on the West Bank of the Jordan. Again, do members of a nation always reside in the same geographical locality as each other under the same political system? Try telling that to Irish Republican Catholics in West Belfast, or to the former residents of East and West Berlin before the Wall came tumbling down, or to the former citizens of the Soviet Union!

Rand's account of what a nation is compares unfavourably with two more nuanced accounts offered by earlier eminent classical liberals. John Stuart Mill once declared,

> A portion of mankind may be said to constitute a Nationality, if they are united among themselves by common sympathies, which do not exist between them and any others—which makes them co-operate with each other more willingly than with other people, desire to be under the same government, and desire that it should be government by themselves or a portion of themselves exclusively.[4]

Likewise, Henry Sidgwick once observed,

> [W]hat is really essential ... to a Nation is ... that the persons composing it should have a consciousness of belonging to one another, of being members of one body, over and above what they derive from the mere fact of being under one government; so that, if their government were destroyed by war or revolution, they would still hold firmly together.[5]

These accounts of Mill and Sidgwick of what a nation is bring out clearly a vital fact about them which Rand's account obscures from view. This is that some people's

forming a nation is above all a function of their consciousness and will. It is not enough to form a nation that a people
reside together in the same territory under the same
government. In addition, they have at least got to *want* so
to live as well. Not even this desire might be sufficient to
make a nation out of a group of people residing together in
a territory under no governance but that of themselves or a
representative of themselves. Beyond having the desire and
opportunity to live as one, to be a nation a people must also
share sufficient mutual affinity to be able to succeed in this
endeavour should they seek to do so. For guidance on how
much mutual affinity a people needs to be a nation, I
propose we turn to the treatment given to this subject by
William McDougall in his ground-breaking 1920 classic
work of social psychology, *The Group Mind.* Despite its off-
putting and misleading title, this work remains, I believe,
one of the best but strangely neglected works on the subject
of nationalism and one that repays close study by classical
liberals and libertarians alike.

McDougall contended there to be no less than seven
separate conditions which a people must satisfy in order
that they could enjoy sufficient mutual affinity to enable
them to live together harmoniously in a territory under the
same government, should they endeavour to do so, and
without satisfying which therefore a people cannot count as
a genuine nation. First, they must possess what McDougall
refers to as a certain degree of *mental homogeneity.*[6]
According to McDougall, this similarity of outlook and
sensibility can result not just from a people sharing a
common culture and physical environment, but also from
their being of the same race as each other. Typically, in
McDougall's view, all such mental homogeneity as distin-
guishes one nationality from another derives in part from
both sources, only the degree of predominance of one or
other of its two contributory sources varying from nation to
nation. Second, to live harmoniously together, a people
must enjoy *freedom of communication.*

> Without ... freedom of communication the various parts of the
> nation cannot become adequately conscious of one another; ... the

idea of the whole must remain very rudimentary in the minds of
the individuals; each part of the whole remains ignorant of many
other parts, and there can be no vivid consciousness of a common
welfare and a common purpose.... [M]ore important[ly] still, there
can be none of that massive influence of the whole upon each of the
units which is the essence of collective mental life.[7]

Among the means of communication which facilitate the
free and reciprocal communication between a people who
reside in any territory larger than that of the city states of
antiquity are the press, radio, telephone, and television, as
well as such mass transportation systems as railroads, cars,
and aeroplanes. However, the prime necessary condition of
the ability of a people to communicate with each other is
fluency in the same language. A third condition of a people's
being able to live harmoniously together is their jointly
possessing the capacity to produce *national leaders*, 'person-
alities of exceptional powers who ... play the part of leaders.[8]
Fourth, there must have been, on occasion at least, a
common well-defined purpose 'present to, and dominant in,
the minds of all individuals.[9] One such occasion is provided
by the need for concerted action on the part of a people to
stave off a threat to their survival or freedom posed by the
prospect of their imminent invasion or conquest by a foreign
power. But war does not provide the only such occasion for
common purpose. A fifth condition of a people being able to
live harmoniously together is their enjoying a sufficient
degree of what Mc Dougall speaks of as *material and formal
continuity*.[10] By 'material continuity' McDougall means a
continuous period of residence in the same territory; and by
'formal continuity' stability and longevity of the major
public institutions which structure their lives. Such continuity is said to be 'an essential presupposition of all the
other main conditions.... On it ... depends the strengths of
custom and tradition and, to a very great extent, the
strength of national sentiment'.[11] Sixth, a people must also
possess some *national self-consciousness*—that is, some
awareness of themselves as being a distinct people. 'Only in
so far as the idea of the people or nation as a whole is
present to the consciousness of individuals and determines
their actions ... [has] a nation in the proper sense of the

word existed'.[12] Finally, a people must feel some sentiment of love or devotion towards that people whom they consider themselves to be. McDougall terms this sentiment *patriotism*.[13] It may be looked on as the well-spring from which all nationalist sentiment and aspiration ultimately derives.

3. Main Contentions

With these preliminaries in place, we may now proceed to consider the degree of compatibility there is between nationalism and liberalism. I intend to answer this question by way of advancing and defending the following three theses.

The first thesis is that, historically speaking, *far from being inherently antagonistic to or subversive of classical liberal ideals and values, nationalism was a* sine qua non *of the initial emergence and realisation of liberal values and ideals.*

My second thesis is that *precisely the very same varieties of nationalism that were historically instrumental in bringing about the birth and partial realisation of classical liberal ideals and values remain a* sine qua non *of their continued and future espousal and realisation.*

My third thesis is that, *at the present time, the greatest threat facing classical liberal ideals and values is posed less by any hostile foreign powers threatening from without those nation states in which these ideals first emerged and in which they have been most fully realised institutionally to date. Rather, it comes from within these states where it assumes the form of powerful political coalitions determined to undermine and ultimately destroy the sense of common nationality of the citizens of these states through replacing it with a heightened sense of their particularity and diversity vis-à-vis each other and which, unless checked, will in time lead to the disintegration of these nations into a mass of contending minorities.*

I shall now attempt to argue briefly for each thesis in turn before concluding by considering and replying to some objections which I can anticipate being raised against them by classical liberals and libertarians.

4. Nationalism as a Condition for the Emergence of Liberalism

Thesis 1: Far from being inherently antagonistic to or subversive of classical liberal ideals and values, nationalism was, historically, a sine qua non of their initial formulation and partial realisation.

In her monumental study tracing the development of national self-consciousness and nationalist sentiment in the five leading nations of the world, Leah Greenfeld has shown in great detail and with enormous perspicacity how classical liberal ideals first came into being in parallel and inextricably interwoven with national self-consciousness and nationalist aspiration in sixteenth-century England, achieving partial realisation there in the following century. Liberal ideals and national awareness are shown to have emerged in tandem in the wake of the political and religious reforms carried out by Henry VIII as a result of his break from Rome.[14] The new self-image which the Protestant English formed of themselves at the time as being a divinely chosen élite gave to them, or, at least, to the relevant sections of them who found representation in the House of Commons, the conceptual resources as well as the motivation to embark in the century after Henry on that protracted struggle against their hereditary rulers which culminated in the Glorious Revolution of 1688. This saw an elected parliament achieve a decisive victory over an hereditary monarchy that had attempted to lay a claim to absolute sovereignty.

As part of the constitutional settlement in which the Crown passed *via* parliamentary decision from the Catholic Stuart line to Protestant William and Mary of Orange and subsequently to the Hanoverians, many of the values and practices which liberals hold dear became enshrined within the English Constitution—albeit, at first, in only a very limited and qualified form. These liberties and practices include liberty of religious worship, equality before the law, freedom of the press, and parliamentary representation.

Well before the English had acquired even this highly qualified degree of religious liberty, but after the desire for it had been awakened during the sixteenth century, sixty-thousand English Puritans, impatient for such freedom, set sail for the new world to create there a New England in which they would be able to enjoy the freedom of worship denied them at home. Those Englishmen and their descendants formed the nucleus of that second great liberal people whose awakening to their own nationhood in the eighteenth century brought forth a still greater realisation of classical liberal ideals on the far side of the Atlantic than had previously been accomplished in England by means of the Glorious Revolution.

The Puritan settlers brought with them to America the same love of liberty which had become a distinctive part of the English national character. They made this love of liberty as equally a distinctive feature of the American nation as it had become of the English nation. As Greenfeld remarks, 'it was through the Puritan mediation that love of liberty became the distinguishing characteristic of America'.[15] Eventually, as in England, this love of liberty among the American settlers became secularised and generalised.[16]

Devotion to this same value of liberty led the American colonists in the eighteenth century to break away from their mother country. By establishing their own independent republic, they became able to enjoy the same self-governance which the English had long regarded as their birthright but which their mother-country had become seemingly intent on denying the colonists. Greenfeld claims as by far the most important factor leading to American independence:

> the fact that Americans had a national identity from the very start and that was the English national identity.... The English idea of the nation implied the symbolic elevation of the common people to the position of an elite, which in theory made every individual the sole legitimate representative of his own interests and an equal participant in the political life of the collectivity.[17]

In the course of defending the moral legitimacy of the American colonists' efforts to throw off the yoke of their mother country, Thomas Paine was led to extend the right

to liberty to all mankind, inviting lovers of liberty everywhere to join the American nation.

> Europe, and not England, is the parent country of America. This
> new world has been the asylum for the persecuted lovers of civil
> and religious liberty from *every part* of Europe.... We claim
> brotherhood with every European Christian, and triumph in the
> generosity of the sentiment.[18]

We might today be less than fully impressed by the liberal-
ity of sentiment here expressed, but its general liberal tenor
remains clear. As Greenfeld put it, the American Revolution
brought into the world the idea that 'self-government is
mankind's birthright, not an English liberty'.[19]

5. Nationalism Still a Sine Qua Non of Liberalism

*Thesis 2: Precisely the same varieties of nationalism that
were historically instrumental in bringing about the birth
and partial realisation of classical liberal ideals and values
remain a* sine qua non of *their continued and future espousal and realisation.*

Despite spreading eastwards as well as westwards from
England, classical liberal ideals and values never managed
to take root in political thought and practice anywhere as
firmly as they were able to in England and the United
States. As that great student of nationalism, Hans Kohn,
once observed:

> [The] [m]odern nationalism [that] first took hold in England in the
> seventeenth century and in Anglo-America in the eighteenth
> century ... respected, and was based upon, the individual liberties
> and self-government characteristic of these nations. The rise of
> nationalism in the French Revolution was different. The absolutist
> and centralised French monarchy had set the example for continen-
> tal Europe in the seventeenth and eighteenth centuries; the
> nationalism of the French people continued this form and set the
> model for the centralised European nation-state of the nineteenth
> century. The Napoleonic wars carried the aggressiveness of the new
> nationalism to the four corners of Europe.[20]

It remains true that England and America have approached far closer than any other nations to realising
classical liberal ideals and values. This is so, despite the
severe erosion of the liberal credentials of each during the

twentieth century. This erosion was, of course, the result of their respective flirtations with collectivist ideologies and policies, especially those connected with social democracy and the welfare state. However, given the deep historic embeddedness of liberal ideals in the political constitutions and national imaginations of these two nations, the best historical prospects for liberty still remain with them and still depend on their continued survival in at least as liberal a form as they are in.

Classical liberals, in my opinion, should not write nationalism off as an attitude of mind that in all its forms is always and everywhere uncongenial to their own values and ideals. Afterall, and notwithstanding the collapse of communism, the two great nation-states of Britain and the USA—states in which classical liberal values have been to date most fully, if yet still only incompletely and imperfectly, realised—are but islands of relative liberty in a vast surrounding ocean of far greater illiberalism.

That the best prospects for the eventual complete realisation of liberal ideals and values lie in the continued survival of these two states in a form which depends on each retaining its historic national identity is a claim made by no less a classical liberal thinker than Ludwig von Mises. In a book written and published during the closing stages of the Second World War after allied victory had become assured, Mises issued the following stark warning:

> It would be a fateful mistake to assume that a return to the policies of liberalism abandoned by the civilised nations some decades ago could cure the [present] evils and open the way towards peaceful co-operation of nations and toward prosperity.... [T]he years of antagonism and conflict have left a deep impression on human mentality, which cannot be easily eradicated. They have marked the souls of men, they have disintegrated the spirit of human co-operation, and have engendered hatreds *which can vanish only in centuries*.
>
> Under present conditions the adoption of a policy of outright *laissez faire* and *laissez passer* on the part of the civilised nations of the West would be equivalent to an unconditional surrender to the totalitarians nations.
>
> Take, for instance, the case of migration barriers. Unrestrictedly opening the doors of the Americas, of Australia, and of Western Europe to immigrants would today be the equivalent to opening the

doors to the vanguards of the armies of Germany, Italy and Japan....

[T]he most that can be expected for the immediate future is the separation of the world into two sections: a liberal, democratic, and capitalist West with about one quarter of the total population, and a militarist and totalitarian East embracing the greater part of the earth's surface and population.[21]

The danger which Mises claimed the liberal democracies faced, and that, in his view, made immigration barriers necessary, was a foreseen scale of immigration without these barriers by peoples of vastly different ethnicity, culture, and outlook to the majority populations of the liberal democracies as would radically destabilise and ultimately imperil their viability.

Mises feared that, without strict immigration controls, the host populations would rapidly be turned into national minorities in their own lands by immigrants who, given the numbers in which he supposed they would enter if able, would remain unassimilated and unassimilable.

Mises also thought that, without strict immigration barriers, the host populations would become vulnerable to forms of oppression and persecution at the hands of the new arrivals who would soon come to out-number their hosts. Through being unassimilated, the new arrivals would not, after all, be indisposed to turn to their own sectional advantage any political power that their numerical superiority would in a short time be able to provide them under conditions of representative democracy.

In an earlier work, Mises had identified as being the most important threat facing the preservation of world peace the fear felt by members of these two nations of being swamped by immigrants of remote outlook and nationality to themselves. He wrote:

In the absence of any migration barriers whatsoever, vast hordes of immigrants ... would, it is maintained, ... inundate Australia and America ... in such great numbers that it would no longer be possible to count on their assimilation.... If, in the past, immigrants to America soon adopted the English language and American ways and customs, this was in part due to the fact that they did not come over all at once in such great numbers.... This ... would now change, and there is real danger that the ascendancy—or more correctly, the exclusive dominion—of the Anglo-Saxons in the United States would be destroyed. This is especially to be feared in the case of heavy immigration on the part of the Mongolian peoples of Asia. [22]

Having identified and articulated this fear, Mises went on to endorse it as reasonable. He wrote:

> it cannot be denied that these fears are justified. Because of the enormous power that today stands at the command of the state, a national minority must expect the worst from a majority of a different nationality. As long as the state is granted the vast powers which it has today and which public opinion considers to be its right, the thought of having to live in a state whose government is in the hands of members of a foreign nationality is positively terrifying. It is frightful to live in a state in which at every turn one is exposed to persecution—masquerading under the guise of justice—by a ruling majority. It is dreadful to be handicapped even as a child in school on account of one's nationality and to be in the wrong before every judicial and administrative authority because one belongs to a national minority. [23]

Mises' ultimate long-term solution to this problem was not the strict immigration controls which he later advocated as a temporary expedient after the War. Such barriers to labour mobility do nothing to reduce the gap in living standards between rich and poor peoples—a gap he perceived to be the root of the envy and rancour felt by the latter towards the former which would render unrestricted immigration by the latter so potentially dangerous for the former. What Mises proposed as the only viable solution to the problem of the discrepancy between rich and poor nations was the universal adoption of the classical liberal agenda of minimal government.

> It is clear that no solution of the problem of immigration is possible if one adheres to the ideal of the interventionist state, which meddles in every field of human activity. Only the adoption of the liberal program could make the problem of immigration, which today seem insoluble, completely disappear. [24]

It was with the problem of relations between rich and poor peoples firmly in mind, therefore, that towards the end of this book, he declared that:

> The greatest ideological question that mankind has ever faced ... is the question of whether we shall succeed in creating throughout the world a frame of mind ... [that] can be nothing less than the unqualified, unconditional acceptance of liberalism. Liberal

thinking must permeate all nations, liberal principles must pervade all political institutions, if the prerequisites of peace are to be created and the causes of war eliminated.[25]

In Mises' view, for the USA or UK to remove all immigration barriers, as some libertarians have advocated,[26] even after such governments had first been reduced in size to the minimum, would still not be enough to prevent the danger he foresaw attendant upon mass immigration into these countries by peoples of very different culture and ethnicity to that of majority. According to Mises, even policing and the judicial process are capable of being turned against minorities by members of majorities who perceive the minorities as alien and foreign to themselves. As Mises put it:

Large areas of the world have been settled, not by the members of just one nationality, one race, or one religion, but by a motley mixture of many peoples. As a result of the migratory movements that necessarily follow shifts in the location of production, more new territories are continually being confronted with the problem of a mixed population....

To be a member of a national minority always means that one is a second class citizen.... The citizen who speaks a foreign tongue ... must obey the law; yet he has a feeling that he is excluded from effective participation in shaping the will of the legislative authority or at least that he is not allowed to cooperate in shaping it to the same extent as those whose native tongue is that of the ruling majority. And when he appears before a magistrate or any administrative official as a party to a suit or petition, he stands before men whose political thought is foreign to him because it developed under different ideological influences. [T]he very fact that the members of the minority are required ... to make use of a language foreign to them already handicaps them, seriously in many respects ... when ... on trial.... At every turn, the member of national minority is made to feel that he lives among strangers and that he is, even if the letter of the law denies it, a second-class citizen....

All these disadvantages are felt to be very oppressive even in a state with a liberal constitution in which the activity of the government is restricted to the protection of the life and property of the citizens. But they become intolerable in an interventionist or a socialist state.[27]

What would and should become of nationalist sentiment and immigration barriers in a world all of whose inhabitants have come to share classical liberal ideals and values can doubtless be the subject of fruitful discussion, and doubtless it has a part to play in classical liberal debate. However, the answer to this question should not determine what attitude classical liberals should adopt towards nationalism in an only partial liberal world. So to decide would be analogous to concluding that, since individual states in a liberal world would have no need for a nuclear deterrent, individual states also have no need for such weapons in a deeply illiberal world in which many states already possess them.

6. Hostility to Nationalism as the Current Threat to Liberalism

Thesis 3: At the present time, the greatest threat facing classical liberal ideals and values is posed less by any hostile foreign powers threatening from without those nation states in which these ideals first emerged and in which they have been most fully realised institutionally to date. Rather, it comes from within these states where it assumes the form of powerful political coalitions determined to undermine and ultimately destroy the sense of common nationality of the citizens of these states through replacing it with a heightened sense of their particularity and diversity vis-à-vis each other and which, unless checked, will in time lead to the disintegration of these nations into a mass of contending minorities

We might term the current threat facing liberal regimes *liberal death wish number two,* the first having been the attempt to make themselves socialist, a danger which seems for the present to have abated since the collapse of communism. The political tendency which currently threatens liberalism often goes today under the name 'multiculturalism'. In the case of Britain, *liberal death wish number two* extends beyond the encouragement and cultivation of separate cultural identities of the various ethnic and cultural groups that make up its citizenry. It calls for the dissolution of the body politic itself into the several historic principalities and regions from which it was formed. In addition it calls for the United Kingdom to relinquish its status as a sovereign state through becoming part of an emerging fully federal European Union the illiberal credentials of which are becoming daily ever more apparent.[28]

As has been pointed out by many commentators, such as Arthur Schlesinger[29] and Samuel Huntington,[30] the implementation of the programme favoured by multi-culturalists in the UK and USA would not lead to any greater autonomy for the minorities on whose behalf it is ostensibly pursued. It would lead, rather, to such fragmentation and dissolution of the civic bonds that unite the diverse constituent peoples who comprise these two great nations as are needed to preserve civility between them. The accentuation of ethnic difference at the expense of common culture and common nationality threatens the liberal character of each nation.

The policies favoured by the multi-culturalists, be they encouraging separate schooling to affirmative action in the work-place, pave the way for a dissolution of the common national bonds which unite the diverse ethnic groups in these nations which enable them to live together harmoniously under the same government. In short, the policies of cultural autonomy favoured by many multi-culturalists would lead, not to the multi-cultural pluralist utopia which their starry-eyed proponents promise, but more likely to equivalents to the burning streets of Sarayevo.

6. Conclusion

Classical liberals should neither ignore nor underestimate the value to their cause of American and British nationalism. The political order to which classical liberals aspire —world-wide minimal government—has no chance of seeing the light of day unless the populaces of Britain and the United States continue to remain as liberal as each has long been. The populaces of neither nation-state can do so unless each preserves its own unique and distinct national identity and status. This will be a hard saying for some, since it will seem to many overly restrictive, and, moreover, historically false.

I anticipate some will be inclined to object that the USA and the present-day UK are, not only, as I have claimed them, the most liberal societies in existence today, judged in classical liberal terms, but also, in terms of the ethnic composition of the citizenry of each, are manifestly multi-national or multi-cultural or multi-ethnic.

Neither the USA nor the UK, however, can be cited as examples of a stable and robust multi-national liberal polity. Thus, their viability cannot serve to counter-instantiate the claim that each needs to preserve its national homogeneity to maintain its viability. This is so for two reasons. First, neither state is genuinely multi-national in the relevant sense. Second, to the extent that each has become multi-national today, so is its liberal character under severe threat. It is imperative to realise that, not-withstanding the rhetoric of the multi-culturalists and devolutionists, neither state has been anything but mono-cultural since its inception, and the viability of each has rested on this fact. In fact, certain cultural hegemonic traits—such as English being the official language of each country—are not optional extras that can safely be dis-carded. Rather, the loss of such cultural hegemony is, perhaps, the greatest threat to their remaining liberal nations that each of them faces.

There is a danger that even classical liberals may be led astray here by misinterpreting the scope of certain remarks made by Mises about what is appropriate liberal policy for polyglot territories and coming to suppose his prescriptions apply in the case of the USA and the UK, given their current multi-cultural composition. In writing about what obtains under polyglot conditions, Mises claimed that the state should withdraw completely in terms of what it demands of its citizens *vis-à-vis* the linguistic competence of their children. Specifically, the state should not insist on any one language being the official one, nor even insist on schooling being compulsory. Classical liberals might suppose this policy should also carry over to present day USA and UK. But the conditions which obtained in the former Hapsburg Empire, which was where Mises had in mind when making this proposal, do not obtain in Britain and America. What holds true of it does not apply to them.

Quite the opposite does. In the case of both the UK and USA, the viability of their liberal institutions reduces in proportion as the state encourages and supports cultural and linguistic diversity. The reasons why this is so were given by John Stuart Mill whose views on this subject remain as valid today as they were when he advanced them over a hundred years ago. Mill wrote:

> Free institutions are next to impossible in a country made up of different nationalities. Among a people without fellow-feeling, the united public opinion, necessary to the working of representative government, cannot exist. The influences which form opinions and decide political acts, are different in the different sections of the country. An altogether different set of leaders have the confidence of one part of the country and of the other.
>
> The same books, newspapers, pamphlets, speeches, do not reach them. One section does not know what opinions, or what instigations, are circulating in another. The same incidents, the same acts, the same system of government, affect them in different ways; and each fears more injury to itself from other nationalities, than from the common arbiter, the State. Their mutual antipathies are generally much stronger than jealousy of the government....
>
> For [this] reason, it is in general a necessary condition of free institutions, that the boundaries of government should coincide in the main with those of nationalities.[31]

'But', I can anticipate the objection, 'are not minorities hampered by or oppressed by this demand for national homogeneity? How can such a demand be liberal?' The answer is: minorities are not hampered or oppressed by such a demand, provided—but only provided—the governments of the states in which they reside remain minimal in function, or, at least, are strictly limited. In proportion as government becomes more than minimal, so what might be involved by its demand for national homogeneity becomes oppressive of minorities.

This is because the more extensive government is the greater is the scope for political power being used by ethnic majorities against minorities. This is the great teaching of Mises from his study of nationalism. It is not that liberal polities should not aspire after and seek to maintain national homogeneity. It is, rather, that, where there are substantial minorities within a territory, to be liberal, government should and must become minimal. As Mises observed:

If the administrative authorities have the right to intervene everywhere according to their discretion, if the latitude granted to judges and officials in reaching their decisions is so wide as to leave room for the operation of political prejudices, then a member of a national minority finds himself delivered over to arbitrary judgement and oppression on the part of the public functionaries belonging to the ruling majority[32]

It is not illiberal for Britain and the United States to keep English the official national language and to demand of parents enjoying permanent residency or citizenship within these countries that they ensure that any children raised there be fluent in English. It would be illiberal for a state to make similar demands which favoured some one natural language in territories which were genuinely polyglot, such as was the former Austro-Hungarian Empire. But neither Britain nor the United States have ever been such.

In genuinely polyglot territories, but only in such, it would be illiberal for the state to make such a demand of its citizens. This is because to do so there is bound to have the effect of alienating children from their parents, the children being instructed in a language different from that which the parents speak. As Mises also observed:

[I]n those extensive areas in which peoples speaking different languages live together side by side intermingled and in polyglot confusion, ... [t]he question of which language is to be made the basis of instruction assumes crucial importance. A decision one way or the other can, over the years, determine the nationality of a whole area. The school can alienate children from the nationality to which their parents belong and be used as a means of oppressing whole nationalities.... In all areas of mixed nationality, the school is a political prize of the highest importance. It cannot be deprived of its political character as long as it remains a public ... institution.[33]

However, those who choose to emigrate to and have been admitted into Britain and America have no right to be granted citizenship, or even permanent residency, while refusing to acquire for themselves, or ensure that their children acquire, the wherewithal to be of that nation. Acquiring fluency in the native tongue is the minimal condition of being able to be such. This is what is so potentially dangerous and divisive about the current multi-cultural movement in both Britain and the United States. In seeking to disunite the citizenry of these two nations, through fostering or even permitting linguistic apartheid, multi-culturalism is sowing the seeds of future disunion and anarchy.[34]

My overall conclusion, therefore, is that, far from being incompatible with or hostile to liberalism, nationalism, of the British and American varieties, is the best friend of liberty and the best guarantor of its survival in the future. This being so, citizens of each who are friends of liberty should affirm and be proud of their liberal and national traditions. They should seek to reverse the terrible decline in national self-esteem that has occurred in recent years in both nations through the ascendancy that has been gained in each of an ideology designed to undermine national-pride and self-esteem out of a misbegotten concern for supposedly disadvantaged minorities.

Lovers of liberty in both nations should be aware and proud of their own liberal national heritages and of the common source from which both spring. So struck was Mises by the affinity between the American and English peoples that in 1919 he went so far as to describe them as forming 'a single nation ... bound by a national bond that will show its binding force in days of great political crisis'.[35]

Accordingly, I shall conclude by articulating a sentiment which I like to think he would have been glad to endorse were he alive today: Long may these two great nations continue to be divided by their common language but united by their distinct, but equally liberal, nationalities!

Notes

1: Why do they come?

1 'UK France and Switzerland', *Migration News*, Vol. 8, No. 3, March 2001, published by Migration Dialogue, University of California Berkeley Center for German and European Studies http://migration.ucdavis.edu/

2 'Organized crime moves into migrant trafficking', in *Trafficking in Migrants*, No. 11, Geneva: International Office for Migration, June 1996. www.iom.int

3 'Detailed costings of an asylum seeker are presently under examination, but if for example we assume that a principal applicant costs around £20,000 p.a. (and this seems a reasonable figure...' *The cost of asylum applications to the United Kingdom 1989-1998*, Harwich: Immigration Service Union Report, p. 4.

4 2002 Asylum Statistics (Applications), London: Home Office.

5 2002 Asylum Statistics (Applications), p. 5.

6 Heath, T. and Hill, R., *Asylum Statistics United Kingdom 2001*, The Home Office Research Development and Statistics Directorate (National Statistics) 31 July 2002, p. 4.

7 Heath and Hill, *Asylum Statistics UK 2001*, 31 July 2002, p. 4.

8 'Britain by the Backdoor', BBC Radio 4, 2001.

9 Popper, K., *The Open Society and Its Enemies*, 1945.

2: The Human Rights Act and the surrender of our borders

1 'Refugees lose home protest', *Daily Telegraph*, 5 December 2002.

2 Dyer, C., 'Woolf warns government over human rights', *Guardian*, 16 October 2002; Rozenberg, J., 'Euro Court Rulings on rights are not binding', *Daily Telegraph*, 16 October 2002.

3 Johnson, P., 'Asylum plans "contain 14 breaches of Human Rights"', *Daily Telegraph*, 22 June 2002

4   Speech by the Foreign Secretary Jack Straw to the United Nations Commission on Human Rights Geneva, 17 April 2002.

5   'Applications for asylum', London: Home Office, 1997, paras. 17 and 18.

6   Bamber, D., *Sunday Telegraph*, 18 August 2002.

7   Report on work of Dr Paddy Rawlinson, an expert on Russian organised crime, *Observer*, 11 February 2001.

8   John Tinsey, Immigration Union spokesman, quoted in *Evening Standard*, 13 February 2001.

9   House of Lords Select Committee on the European Union, 'A Common Policy on Illegal Immigration', HL Paper 187, 5 November 2002, p. 14.

10   'Combatting the experiences of undocumented migrants', Irena Omelaniuk, Director, Migration Management Services, International Office of Migration. Paper given at the 6th International Metropolis Conference, Rotterdam, November 2001.

11   House of Lords Select Committee on the European Union, 'A Common Policy on Illegal Immigration', HL Paper 187, 5 November 2002.

12   Select Committee on Home Affairs, Appendices to minutes of evidence, prepared 31 January 2001, Appendix 7, memorandum by Kent County Constabulary. http.www.parliament-the-stationery-office.uk/pa/cm200001/cmselect/cmhaff/163/163ap37.htm

13   Sapstead, D., 'Tunnel chaos as asylum seekers halt trains', *Daily Telegraph*, 15 May 2002.

14   Coleman, D., 'Migration to Europe: A critique of the new establishment consensus', Network for Integrated European Population Studies, Workshop on Demographic and Cultural Specificity and Integration of Migrants, Bingen, Germany, November 2000, see Working Paper No. 1, http://www.apsoc.ox.ac.uk/oxpop/papers.htm

15   MigrationwatchUK, press release 26 September 2002, 'Work Permits and Immigration', http:www.migrationwatchuk.org/pressreleases_workpermits.asp

3: A brief history of immigration

1 Duffy, J., 'Are the British a race?', BBC News, Friday 20 April 2001. http://news.bbc.co.uk/1/hi/uk/1288231.htm

2 Semino, O., Passarino, G., Oefner, P., Lin, A.A., Arbuzova, S., Beckman, E., Bendictis, Gd., Francalacci, P., Kouvasti, A., Santachiara- Benercetti, S., Cavalli-Sforza, L. and Underhill, P.A., 'The Genetic Legacy of Paleolithic Homo Sapiens in Extant Europeans: A Y Chromosome Perspective', *Science*, 10 November 2000, pp. 1155-59.

3 Renfrew, C., *Archaeology and Language*, Pimlico, 1998, pp. 278-79.

4 Roberts, A., *Eminent Churchillians*, Phoenix Press, 1994, p. 218.

5 Roberts, *Eminent Churchillians*, p. 218.

6 Lewis, R., *Enoch Powell: Principle in Politics*, Cassell, 1979, p. 110.

7 Roberts, *Eminent Churchillians*, p. 224.

8 Roberts, *Eminent Churchillians*, p. 216.

9 Personal communication to the author.

10 Seldon, M., 'Tory Old Party Contemptibles', *Tribune*, 4 May 2001.

11 *Hansard*, 16 June 1971 col. 563; *Hansard*, 11 November 1969 col. 320.

12 Lewis, *Enoch Powell: Principle in Politics*, 1979, pp. 110-11.

13 Carcopino, J., *Daily Life in Ancient Rome*, Penguin, 1991, p. 68.

14 *Birmingham Post*, 22 April 1968.

15 'When the Tiber failed to foam. A Searchlight "depreciation" of one of Britain's most evil postwar politicians', *Searchlight*, 1998.

16 Casart, R. and Shepard, P., 'Human Bondage', Associated Press, Boston, 2 December 2001.

17 'Britain by the Backdoor', BBC Radio 4, 23 December 2001.

18 Personal communication to the author, 1999.

19 Heath, T. and Hill, R., *Asylum Statistics United Kingdom 2001*, The Home Office Research Development and Statistics Directorate (National Statistics) 31 July 2002, p. 4.

20 Mallourides, E. and Turner, G., *Control of Immigration: Statistics United Kingdom, 2001*, Home Office, 26 September 2002, p. 11.

4: How to get in

1   See, for example, Boggan, S., 'Visa Shop Scam', *Evening Standard*, 4 November 2002.

2   *Migration News*, Vol. 8, No. 3, March 2001.

3   'Dublin is Terror Base', *Observer*, 4 August 2002.

4   'Butcher of Sierra Leone', *The Times*, 16 September 2000.

5   'Refugees—ask the expert', interview with Harriet Sergeant, BBC Radio News, 25 June 2002.

6   Mallourides, E. and Turner, G., *Control of Immigration: Statistics United Kingdom, 2001*, Home Office, 26 September 2002, p. 3.

7   MigrationwatchUK, 'The "Primary Purpose" Rule', see 'Other documents' at website: www.migrationwatchuk.org

8   Dalrymple, T., 'The abuse of women', The *Spectator*, 27 October 2001.

9   'Blunkett defends marriage comments', BBC News Online, 8 February 2002. http://news.bbc.co.uk/1/hi/uk_politics/1807885.stm

10 'Blunkett defends marriage comments', 2002.

11 Alibhai Brown, Y., 'The secrets and lies of Britain's Asians', *Independent*, 15 July 2002.

12 Dunne, M., 'Women fight back: Southall Black Sisters raise a fist', Third World Network, 8 June 1997. http://www.hartford-hwp.com/archives/61/061.htm

13 'Police act on forced marriages', BBC World Service Education, Tuesday January 16 2001. http://news.bbc.co.uk/1/hi/uk/1119008.stm

14 Stobart, E., *Dealing with cases of forced marriage: Guidelines for police*, Association of Chief Police Officers and the Foreign and Commonwealth Office, 2000, p. 2.

15 Farrell, S., 'Seven weddings and a court case for lapdancer', *The Times*, 5 November 1998.

5: How to stay

1 'Third Country Cases', Law and Policy, Chapter 4, Section 2, Immigration and Nationality Directorate, the Home Office. www.workpermits.gov.uk/default.asp?pageid=2654

2 *Migration News*, Vol. 4, No. 6, June 1997.

3 Johnston, P., 'France and Germany Unsafe for Refugees', *Daily Telegraph*, 20 December 2000.

4 'Asylum plans contain 14 breaches of human rights', *Daily Telegraph*, 22 June 2002.

5 MigrationwatchUK, Bulletin No. 2, 2002.

6 The World Socialist Web Site: http:/64.65.0.153/cgi-bin/search/search/.pl Extract from book, *A State Murder Exposed*, 1998, ISBN 1- 873045-123.

7 *Hansard*, 7 February 2002, col. 1075.

8 Beverley Hughes MP, quoted in Travis, A., 'Iraqis head list as asylum figures rise', *Guardian*, 31 August 2002.

9 MigrationwatchUK, Bulletin No. 1, 11 June 2002, p. 3.

6: The tribunals

1 Worldwide Refugee Information: Country Report: France, U.S. Committee for Refugees, http://preview.refugees.org/world/countryrpt/europe/2001/france.htm

2 'Too many convicts', leader in *The Economist*, 10 August 2002, p. 13.

3 'Control of Unscrupulous Immigration Advisers', Lord Chancellor's Department, January 1998.

7: Counting them in

1   Bright, M. and Veash, N., 'Britain shelters more refugees', *Observer*, 22 November 1998.

2   Browne, A., 'UK Whites will be a minority in Britain by 2100', *Observer*, 3 September 2000.

3   Commission on the Future of Multi-Ethnic Britain, *The Future of Multi-Ethnic Britain (The Parekh Report)*, London: Profile Books, 2000, p. 14, epigraph to chapter 2, 'Rethinking the National Story'.

4   *The Future of Multi-Ethnic Britain*, 2000, p. 57, epigraph to chapter 5, 'Dealing with Racisms',

5   MigrationwatchUK, Bulletin No. 7, 30 July 2002.

6   MigrationwatchUK, Bulletin No. 2, 23 June 2002.

7   'Overview', MigrationwatchUK, www.migrationwatch.org

8   Sergeant, H., *'Welcome to the Asylum': Immigration and Asylum in the UK*, London: Centre for Policy Studies, 2001, p. 14.

9   Sergeant, *Welcome to the Asylum*, 2001, pp. 14-15.

10   Home Office, evidence, Appendix 1, para 9.4, cited in Select Committee on Home Affairs - First Report, published on 23 January 2001. http://www.parliament.the-stationery-office.co.uk/pa/ cm200001/cmselect/cmhaff/163/16305.htm

11   *The Sunday Times*, 14 April 2002.

12   Personal witness statement to author 2001.

13   *The Times*, 7 May 2002.

14   Private communication, 2002.

15   'The Cost of Asylum Applications to the United Kingdom 1989-1998', Harwich: Immigration Service Union, undated, p. 6.

16   'The Cost of Asylum Applications to the United Kingdom 1989-1998', undated.

17   National Audit Office, Community Legal Service: The introduction of contracting, HC89 Session 2002-2003, 28 November 2002, pp. 7-8.

18 'The Cost of Asylum Applications to the United Kingdom 1989-1998', p. 8.

19 'The Cost of Asylum Applications to the United Kingdom 1989-1998', p. 8.

8: Deportation: bailing with a colander

1 *Daily Express*, 30 July 2001.

2 Mallourides, E. and Turner, G., *Control of Immigration: Statistics United Kingdom 2001*, Home Office, 26 September 2002, p. 13

3 Mallourides and Turner, *Control of Immigration: Statistics United Kingdom 2001*, 2002, p. 13.

4 Harris, P. and Byrne, N., 'Arson, abuse, stone-throwing: Ireland's welcome for refugees', *Guardian Unlimited*, Sunday 19 August 2001. http://society.guardian.co.uk/asylumseekers/story/0,7991,539650,00.html

5 Mahoney, D., 'Asylum seekers live in fear of ejection after Ireland strikes £7 million pound deal', *Scotland on Sunday*, 19 August 2001; Byrne, N., 'Refugee deal', *Observer*, 12 August 2001; Nwosu, N. and Ogunsakin, M., 'Court urged to restrain government on Repatriation Act with Ireland', the *Guardian Lagos*, http://allafrica.com 29 August 2001.

6 Mahoney, 'Asylum seekers live in fear of ejection after Ireland strikes £7m pound deal', *Scotland on Sunday*, 19 August 2001.

7 Clarke, M., 'Legal Aid for Asylum Seekers Doubles - Asylum Gravy Train', *Daily Mail*, 9 May 2002.

8 Walsh, B., 'The Men Making Millions from Refugees' Misery', *Observer*, 2 September 2001, p. 6.

9 Oxfam Policy Papers, 'Summary report of Submission papers to Home Office on asylum vouchers', December 2000.

10 'Six months after September 11, hijackers' visa approval received', Potter, M. and Phillips, R., CNN Miami Bureau, 13 March 2002.

11 Milward, M., 'Insurance veto closes Yarlswood', *Daily Telegraph*, week of 3 April 2002.

9: Why immigration should be controlled

1 'Organised Illegal Immigration', National Criminal Intelligence Service, 28 June 2000. http://www.ncis.co.uk/PRESS/24_00.asp

2 United Nations, *Replacement Migration: Is it a Solution to Declining and Ageing Populations?*, New York: United Nations, 2000.

3 Coleman, D., 'Migration to Europe: A critique of the new establishment consensus', Network for Integrated European Population Studies, Workshop on Demographic and Cultural Specificity and Integration of Migrants, Bingen, Germany, November 2000, see Working Paper Nó. 1, http://www.apsoc.ox.ac.uk/oxpop/papers.htm

4 *Population Trends 101*, London: Office for National Statistics, Autumn 2000, p. 13.

5 Pankaj, V., *Family Mediation Services for Minority Ethnic Families in Scotland*, Scottish Executive Research Unit, Edinburgh: The Stationery Office, 2000, 9:1, 'changing attitudes of second/third generation'; Penn, R. and Lambert, P., 'Ethnic/Nationality Group Attitudes Towards Ideal Family Size in Britain, France and Germany', European Population Conference, 2001, Helsinki, Finland 7-9 June 2001, Theme E: International Migration and Migrant Populations.

6 Coleman, 'Migration to Europe: A critique of the new establishment consensus', November 2000. http://www.apsoc.ox.ac.uk/oxpop/papers.htm

7 'Blunkett admits huge asylum overspend', BBC News, 2 June 2002. http://news.bbc.co.uk/1/hi/uk_politics/2021746.stm

8 Coleman, 'Migration to Europe: A critique of the new establishment consensus', November 2000, p. 6. http://www.apsoc.ox.ac.uk/oxpop/papers.htm

9 Coleman, D., 'Population Ageing: an unavoidable future', *Social Biology and Human Affairs*, 66, pp. 1-11; see also Working Paper No. 7, http://www.apsoc.ox.ac.uk/oxpop/papers.htm

10 Coleman, 'Migration to Europe: A critique of the new establishment consensus', November 2000. http://www.apsoc.ox.ac.uk/oxpop/papers.htm

11 Gove, M., 'It's good for them, and better for the rest of us', *The Times*, 30 April 2002.

12 Coleman, 'Migration to Europe: A critique of the new establishment consensus', November 2000. http://www.apsoc.ox.ac.uk/oxpop/papers.htm

10: Law Reform

1 Immigration Law Update, Ahmed v SSHD 'Evidence probative value genuineness of documents', Legal Research Unit of the Immigration Advisory Service, 4 April 2002, pp. 5-7.

2 Immigration Law Update, Ndiritu, 'Burden of proof', Legal Research Unit of the Immigration Advisory Service, 17 April 2002, pp. 1-2.

3 Immigration Law Update, 'Human rights extra territorial effect', articles 3,5,6,8, Legal Research Unit of the Immigration Advisory Service.

4 Craven, N. and Butler, J., 'Satellite TV, Disney videos, pocket money and free clothes', *Daily Mail*, 14 September 2002.

5 Rozenberg J. and Johnson, P., 'Deportation of Afghan family ruled illegal', *Daily Telegraph*, 12 September 2002.

6 'British government to crack down on illegal workers', Workpermit.com, January 2002.

7 Personal communication.

Nationalism and Liberalism
David Conway

1 Hayek, F., *The Constitution of Liberty*, London: Routledge and Kegan Paul, 1960, pp. 14-15.

2 Hayek, *The Constitution of Liberty*, p. 405.

3   Rand, A., 'Don't Let It Go', (1971) in Rand, A.,
    Philosophy: Who Needs It, New York: Signet, 1984,
    p. 205.

4   Mill, J.S., 'Considerations on Representative
    Government', (1859) in Gray, J. (ed.), Mill, J.S., *On
    Liberty and Other Essays*, Oxford and New York:
    Oxford University Press, 1991, p. 427.

5   Sidgwick, H., *Elements of Politics*, London and New
    York: Macmillan, 1891, p. 214.

6   McDougall, W., *The Group Mind*, Cambridge:
    Cambridge University Press, 1920, p. 107.

7   McDougall, *The Group Mind*, 1920, p. 132.

8   McDougall, *The Group Mind*, 1920, p. 135.

9   McDougall, *The Group Mind*, 1920, p. 142.

10 McDougall, *The Group Mind*, 1920, p. 145.

11 McDougall, *The Group Mind*, 1920, p. 145.

12 McDougall, *The Group Mind*, 1920, p. 158.

13 McDougall, *The Group Mind*, 1920, p. 164.

14 'In the sixteenth century England underwent a
    profound social transformation.... [F]irst, ... [came] the
    extinction of the old nobility ... complete[d] by 1540....
    Simultaneously with the destruction of the old nobility,
    a stratum destined to replace it appeared. The new—
    Henrician—aristocracy ... was predominantly an official
    elite.... [T]he majority ... were people of modest birth ...
    recruited from the minor gentry or even humbler
    strata. The aristocracy ... became open to talent.... A
    fundamental transformation of this kind ... required a
    rationalisation and justification.... *It is at this juncture
    ... that nationalism was born.* The idea of the nation—
    of the people as an elite—appealed to the new aristo-
    cracy.... In a way, nationality made every Englishman a
    nobleman.... By the 1530s ... entering the discourse ...
    [was the] concept of England as a separate entity and
    as a polity which was not simply a royal patrimony but
    a commonwealth.... [A]lso under Henry ... another
    factor appeared the implications of which for both the
    development and the nature of English nationalism
    were enormous.... Henry's break from Rome ... opened
    the doors to Protestantism, perhaps the most signif-

icant among the factors that furthered the development of ... English national consciousness.... The Protestant insistence on the priesthood of all believers reinforced the rationalist individualism in which the idea of the nation in England was grounded.... The reading of the Bible planted and nurtured among the common people in England a novel sense of human—individual—dignity, which was instantly to become one of their dearest possessions.... For the newly acquired sense of dignity made masses of Englishmen a part of that small circle of new aristocrats and clergymen ... who were already enchanted by the idea of the people as an elite, and of themselves as members of such a people'. Greenfeld, L., *Nationalism: Five Roads to Modernity*, Cambridge, Mass. and London: 1992, pp. 47-54, *passim*.

15 Greenfeld, *Nationalism: Five Roads to Modernity*, 1992, p. 407.

16 'As in England, godliness in the colonies gradually acquired a secular meaning, which by the eighteenth century—[had] bec[o]me dominant and [which], even more than in England, expressed itself in devotion to the triad—liberty, equality and reason.... American society was exemplary in its devotion to the English ideals: it turned them into reality.... The sense of exemplary devotion to and implementation of English values was shared by the colonists everywhere and became a central element in the local American identity.' Greenfeld, *Nationalism: Five Roads to Modernity*, 1992, pp. 408-9.

17 Greenfeld, *Nationalism: Five Roads to Modernity*, 1992, p. 420.

18 Paine, T., *Common Sense* (1776), Harmondsworth: Penguin Books, 1976, pp. 84-85.

19 Greenfeld, *Nationalism: Five Roads to Modernity*, 1992.

20 Kohn, H., 'Nationalism', in De Crespigny, A. and Cronin, J. (eds), *Ideologies of Politics*, Capetown, London and New York: Oxford University Press, p. 156.

21 Mises, L., *Omnipotent Government: The Rise of the Total State and Total War*, Spring Mills, PA: Libertarian Press, 1969, pp. 10-11.

22 Mises, L., *Liberalism in the Classical Tradition*, New York and San Francisco: Foundation for Economic Education Inc. and Cobden Press, 1985, pp. 141-42.

23 Mises, *Liberalism in the Classical Tradition*, pp. 141-42.

24 Mises, *Liberalism in the Classical Tradition*, p. 142.

25 Mises, *Liberalism in the Classical Tradition*, p. 150.

26 See Simon, J.L., *Population Matters*, New Brunswick and London: Transaction Publishers, 1990.

27 Mises, *Liberalism in the Classical Tradition*, pp. 117-20, *passim*.

28 For an elaboration of this thesis, see Conway, D., 'The Future of Liberty in the European Union', *The European Journal*, Vol. 8, N. 6, May 2001.

29 See Schlesinger, A.M., *The Disuniting of America: Reflections on a Multicultural Society*, New York and London: W.W. Norton and Co., 1992.

30 Huntington, S.P., *The Clash of Civilizations and the Remaking of World Order*, London, New York, Sydney, Tokyo, Toronto, Singapore: Touchstone Books, 1996.

31 Mill, 'Considerations on Representative Government', in Gray, 1991, pp.428-30.

32 Mises, *Liberalism in the Classical Tradition*, p. 120.

33 Mises, *Liberalism in the Classical Tradition*, p. 116.

34 Some might wonder whether the cause of liberty is not best served today by the US and UK taking the path some would advocate of ever greater cultural and political regional autonomy, eventually issuing in the dissolution of these political unions through secession from them of whichever constituent states or confederations chose through referenda to secede. My view is that the cause of liberty remains unaffected one way or the other no matter how zealously cultural or even political regional autonomy might be pursued in these political confederations. This is provided the manner of

its pursuit and the exercise of any such autonomy acquired remains, as is conceivable but unlikely, consistent with upholding the civil and political rights of any dissenting cultural minorities resident within those regions. However, it is highly anachronistic to suppose that secession today in either state is anywhere desired by any regional majority, or, if, say, as in Northern Ireland, it was, it is capable of coming about without a form of 'ethnic cleansing' that renders it unconscionable to classical liberals. This issue is as huge as it is important and I cannot here give it the extended attention it merits. For a very interesting set of discussions on the subject, many of which express views very different to my own, see Gordon, D. (ed.), *Secession, State, & Liberty*, New Brunswick and London: Transaction Publishers, 1998.

35 Mises, L., *Nation, State, and Economy*, New York and London: New York University Press, 1983, p. 19.